BARRON'S

W9-AWV-770

1001 PITFALLS IN *Spanish*

Third Edition

Marion P. Holt
College of Staten Island
City University of New York

Julianne Dueber
Parkway South High School
St. Louis, Missouri

Barron's Educational Series, Inc.

All inquiries should be addressed to:
Barron's Educational Series, Inc.
250 Wireless Boulevard
Hauppauge, New York 11788

Library of Congress Catalog Card No. 96-85088

International Standard Book No. 0-8120-9650-9

PRINTED IN THE UNITED STATES OF AMERICA
987654321

CONTENTS

PREFACE

1001 Pitfalls in Spanish is designed as a reference book and self-help guide for high school and college students. Although it deals especially with matters of grammar, style, and choice of vocabulary that are typical and perennial stumbling blocks for the inexperienced language learner, students at all levels will find this book useful as a source of information on correct contemporary usage of Spanish. Some teachers may also find it a practical supplementary text for specialized courses that focus on composition or translation. Many have used it to prepare students for the Advanced Placement Spanish Language Examination.

Throughout the text, the emphasis is on basic concepts and their corresponding "pitfalls," or exceptions. It deals first with the basic parts of speech, then moves to the complexities of professional terminology. For the sake of conciseness and easy reading, we have labeled as "pitfalls" only those constructions and situations that have been the most troublesome in our own experience, or that are sometimes overlooked in classes in which grammar presentation is minimized. However, as the title of the book indicates, the solutions to literally hundreds of additional language pitfalls are presented in a manner designed to aid the serious student of limited experience. An index indicates where each point of usage is discussed.

The third edition of *1001 Pitfalls in Spanish* retains all of the basic features of the first and second editions, but we have updated examples or substituted new ones in some instances. Many of our examples are based on models found in contemporary Spanish and Spanish American novels, plays, newspapers, and magazines, and they will introduce to the reader a number of new and useful words. Also, a few grammatical explanations have been modified or clarified to reflect current usage. Recognizing the increased importance of computers both in professional and personal activities, we have added a new vocabulary for computers and their applications. The vocabularies of the most frequently used words in medicine, banking, law enforcement and other fields have been reviewed and refined.

A special feature of *1001 Pitfalls in Spanish* is its approach to grammar and words from the viewpoint of English-speaking students to enable them to comprehend and to resolve the difficulties that confront them by means of direct comparison with their dominant language. Sometimes what seems self-evident to one will cause difficulties for another, and for that reason no problem of basic usage has been regarded as too insignificant for consideration. Descriptions and explanations avoid specialized terms, which may not be familiar to many students, in favor of simple, direct language easily understood by all. Where language terms other than those regularly employed for treating grammar and words (i.e. noun, adjective, verb, subjunctive, etc.) occur, they are clearly defined.

In many instances, common student errors are shown with the corrections, but these typical examples of incorrect usage—drawn in part from actual student compositions—are presented in such a way that the reader will remember the correct and not the incorrect model. An argument for the demonstration of typical mistakes is the need to reinforce the idea that students must avoid the literal translation of English into Spanish, which leads to so many incorrect or absurd sentences. This type of comparison is appropriate and, indeed, highly useful in a reference work whose function is to guide, caution, and answer questions in the absence of a teacher and to supplement the customary materials used in the classroom.

Although we have sought to avoid imitation or duplication of other works on the Spanish language, we have consulted standard reference and teaching sources in the preparation of this edition. The bibliography has been revised and updated to include recent publications on usage and the most comprehensive Spanish and Spanish-English dictionaries currently available.

Marion P. Holt

Julianne Dueber

PARTS OF SPEECH

1 Adjectives

ADJECTIVES

Adjectives are words that describe or identify a person or thing (tall —*alto*, famous—*famoso*, red—*rojo*, handsome—*guapo*). Some types of adjectives simply limit or point out the word they modify (third— *tercero*, this—*este*), other adjectives indicate the possessor (my—*mi*, your—*tu*), and a few serve to indicate the non-existence of a noun (no—*ninguno*) or to phrase a question about a noun (which—*qué*, how much—*cuánto*).

TYPES OF ADJECTIVES

Descriptive or Qualifying Adjectives

A descriptive adjective characterizes a noun by giving it a distinguishing quality. In the sentence: *Déme usted la corbata roja*, the speaker is answering the probable question: *¿Cuál de estas corbatas quiere usted?* The adjective *roja* identifies and sets the tie off from other ties of different colors.

——————————————— RULE ———————————————

In the example above it would be possible to reply to the question without actually using the noun *corbata*: *Déme usted la roja*. But it would not be correct to include the word "one" as the English-speaker is inclined to do. English: Give me the red one.

1

INCORRECT	**Déme usted la roja una.**
CORRECT:	***Déme usted la roja.***

ADJECTIVES AND AGREEMENT

───────────────── RULE ─────────────────

Unlike English, the Spanish adjective must be made plural if the noun it modifies is plural; and adjectives ending in *o*, as well as those in certain special categories, must also show agreement of gender (masculine or feminine).

M. Sing.	**el apartamento pequeño** the small apartment
M. Plur.	**los apartamentos pequeños** the small apartments
F. Sing.	**la alcoba pequeña** the small bedroom
M. Plur.	**las alcobas pequeñas** the small bedrooms

Compare the variations of the Spanish "pequeño" with the unchanging English "small." (See also section on *Position of Adjectives*.)

───────────────── RULE ─────────────────

Most adjectives that end in a consonant or a vowel other than *o* have the same form for masculine and feminine; the plural of adjectives ending in a consonant normally add *es* to form the plural; those ending in a vowel add *s*.

M. Sing.	**el coche verde** the green car
M. Plur.	**los coches verdes** the green cars

F. Sing.	la camisa verde the green shirt
F. Plur.	las camisas verdes the green shirts
M. Sing.	el número superior the higher number
M. Plur.	los números superiores the higher numbers
F. Sing.	la puerta interior the inner door
F. Plur.	las puertas interiores the inner doors

PITFALL

However, adjectives that end in *án, ín, ón,* or *dor* add *a* to show feminine agreement.

Es un señor muy hablador.
He's a very talkative gentleman.

Es una señora muy habladora.
She's a very talkative lady.

PITFALL

When an adjective ending in *z* is made plural, the *z* is changed to *c* before the *es* plural ending.

Feliz Navidad
Merry Christmas

Felices Pascuas
Happy Holidays

PITFALL

Feminine adjectives of nationality or origin must show feminine agreement even though the masculine form ends in a consonant.

el embajador japonés
the Japanese ambassador

la cantante japonesa
the Japanese singer

los autores españoles
the Spanish authors

PITFALL

An adjective that describes **two or more** nouns of different genders is masculine plural. The masculine noun should appear *last*.

la novela y el cuento modernos
the modern novel and short story

PITFALL

An adjective that describes **two or more** feminine nouns must be feminine plural.

la sociedad y la política contemporáneas
contemporary society and politics

PITFALL

When **plural** nouns denoting units are modified by **more than one** adjective, the adjectives will agree in gender but will be singular.

los idiomas español y portugués
the Spanish and Portuguese languages (only *two* languages are being considered)

los soldados francés y americano
the French and American soldiers (one soldier of each nationality)

los soldados franceses y americanos
the French and American soldiers (two large groups)

POSITION OF ADJECTIVES

In English it is normal and expected that a descriptive adjective will precede the word it modifies. *In Spanish the position of the adjective is more frequently postnominal—that is, following the modified noun.* (However, in certain instances the Spanish adjective does precede the noun.)

English: (normal)   a marvelous night

Spanish: (normal)   **una noche maravillosa**

—————————— RULE ——————————

Adjectives of classification and nationality **must** follow the noun (or nouns) in Spanish.

English: It is a literary work of the Golden Age.

Spanish: **Es una obra literaria del Siglo de Oro.**

English: He's the Russian ambassador to the United States.

Spanish: **Es el embajador ruso a los Estados Unidos.**

—————————— RULE ——————————

Any adjectives modified by adverbs **must** follow the noun that is described.

adv.   adj.   noun

English: Fuentes is a very important writer.

A literal translation of English word order here would result in an awkward and incorrect sentence in Spanish:

INCORRECT SPANISH: **Fuentes es un muy importante escritor.**

noun   adv.   adj.

↓   ↓   ↓

CORRECT SPANISH: *Fuentes es un escritor muy importante.*

PITFALL

Descriptive adjectives that normally follow the noun are placed before the noun when they indicate an expected or inseparable characteristic of the word described.

the red blood	**la roja sangre**
the white snow	**la blanca nieve**
famous movie stars	**famosas estrellas del cine**
the small screen (TV)	**la pequeña pantalla**

PITFALL

In poetry descriptive adjectives are sometimes placed before the noun to achieve an effect desired by the poet.

"*Gigante voz* que el caos ordena en el cerebro . . ."

                (Gustavo Adolfo Bécquer, Rima LII)

But:

"*Olas gigantes* que os rompéis bramando . . ."

                      (Bécquer, Rima III)

PITFALL

The meanings of certain adjectives depend on whether the adjective precedes or follows the noun modified:

	Before the Noun	After the Noun
	(Figurative Meaning)	(Literal Meaning)
antiguo	old, former	old, ancient
algún(o)	some	any at all
bajo	low, vile	short, low
caro	dear (beloved)	expensive, costly

cierto	a certain	sure, definite
dichoso	disagreeable, annoying	lucky, fortunate
gran, grande	great	large (size)
medio	half	average
mismo	same, very	himself (herself, etc)
nuevo	another, new	new, brand new
pobre	unfortunate	poor (without money)
propio	own	proper, suitable
raro	rare (few)	strange, odd
único	only	unique
viejo	old (long-time)	old (elderly)

No puedo soportar su *dichoso* acordeón.
I can't stand his *annoying (confounded) accordion*.

El *hombre dichoso* es el que sabe hacer felices a los demás.
The *lucky (blessed) man* is the one who knows how to make his fellow man happy.

Cierto señor de Alicante ganó el premio gordo.
A *certain man* from Alicante won the grand prize.

Tendrá un *éxito cierto* con esta comedia.
He'll have a *sure success* with this play.

Limiting Adjectives

Limiting adjectives single out one or more persons or things from others of the same category (the, that, those, many, some, etc.) or indicate numerical quantity or rank (twenty, fifth). They provide no descriptive information.

ARTICLES

An article is the most frequent adjective in Spanish. The definite article denotes a definite person, place, or thing (LA *mujer*—the woman, EL *edificio*—the building). The indefinite article modifies an indefinite person or thing (UN *joven*—a youth, UNA *casa*—a house).

7

Unlike English, the Spanish articles show agreement with the accompanying noun.

THE DEFINITE ARTICLE

Forms of the Definite Article:

Masculine singular	— **el coche**	the car
Masculine plural	— **los coches**	the cars
Feminine singular	— **la carta**	the letter
Feminine plural	— **las cartas**	the letters

PITFALL

The masculine article *el* must be used with singular feminine nouns beginning with a stressed *a* or *ha*. (This makes the combination easier to pronounce.) In the plural, however, the same nouns take the normal feminine *las*. (The *s* separates the *a*'s.)

el agua	the water	but	**las aguas**	the waters
el águila	the eagle		**las águilas**	the eagles
el hacha	the axe		**las hachas**	the axes

PITFALL

The preposition **a + the masculine singular article** *el* becomes *al*, and the preposition *de + el* becomes *del*. These are the only contractions in Spanish.

Van al teatro.
They're going to the theater.

Es la casa del presidente.
It's the president's house.

Note, however, that such contractions may not occur when the article is part of a proper name.

La casa de El Greco
The house of El Greco

San Lorenzo de El Escorial
(the town where the Escorial is located)

SPECIAL USES OF THE DEFINITE ARTICLE IN SPANISH

PITFALL

The definite article is used before names of languages **except** after the preposition *en* (and sometimes *de*) and the verb *hablar.* (Occasionally the article is omitted after other verbs whose meaning indicates some use of the language.)

Es un libro de español.
It's a Spanish book (i.e., for teaching Spanish).

Es un texto español.
It's a Spanish textbook (i.e., printed in Spain—perhaps for teaching history).

Este documento está escrito en francés.
This document is written in French.

Creo que están hablando portugués.
I think they're speaking Portuguese.

No me gusta estudiar alemán.
I don't like to study German.

But:

Mis amigos hablan bien el catalán.
My friends speak Catalan well.
(The adverb *bien* stands between *hablar* and the language, and the article is required.)

El italiano es un idioma muy suave.
Italian is a very soft language.

PITFALL

The definite article is used before most titles except in **direct address.**

> **No conozco al señor Gómez.**
> I don't know Mr. Gómez.
>
> **El profesor Alonso es muy famoso.**
> Professor Alonso is very famous.
>
> **¿Como está usted, señor Gómez?**
> How are you, Mr. Gómez?

PITFALL

In colloquial Spanish the article is sometimes used with **first** names, but this practice should not be imitated.

Colloquial: **La Paca, El Gregorio,** etc.

Note, however, that certain famous personalities acquire nicknames that include the article and that are better known than the original names of the individuals. (*El Cordobés* (bullfighter), *El Greco* (painter), *La Argentina* (dancer), etc.)

—————————————— RULE ——————————————

The definite article is not used with the titles *don, doña, fray, San, Santo, Santa,* and *sor.*

> **Don Juan Tenorio fue el burlador de Sevilla.**
> Don Juan Tenorio was the trickster of Seville.
>
> **Fray Luis de León fue un poeta del siglo diez y seis.**
> Fray (Friar) Luis de León was a poet of the sixteenth century.

PITFALL

The definite article is used with parts of the **body** and **clothing** in lieu of the possessive adjective.

Debes ponerte el impermeable cuando está lloviendo.
You should put on your raincoat when it's raining.

Me lavé la cara.
I washed my face.

Los estudiantes levantaron la mano.
The students raised their hands.

(Each raised one hand. If *la mano* became *las manos*, it would mean that each student raised both hands.)

PITFALL

The definite article is used before names of the **days of the week** instead of *en* to translate the English "on."

Llegarán el viernes.
They'll arrive on Friday.

Van a la iglesia los domingos.
They go to church on Sundays.

Note, however, that the article is not used after any form of the verb *ser*, since in such cases this verb is the equivalent of the English "equals."

Hoy es domingo.
Today is Sunday.

Ayer fue sábado.
Yesterday was Saturday.

─────────────── RULE ───────────────

Before nouns of a general or abstract nature, the definite article is required in Spanish, whereas in English the noun stands alone.

Así es *la vida*.
Such is life.

Me gusta *la música.*
I like music (in general).

En este país se usa mucho *la aerofotografía.*
Aerial photography is used a great deal in this country.

El hombre **es víctima de sus circunstancias.**
Man (in general) is the victim of his circumstances.

PITFALL

Note, however, that we occasionally find abstract or general nouns without the article in titles of **literary works.**

Paz en la guerra
Peace in War (Unamuno)

Sangre y arena
Blood and Sand (Blasco Ibáñez)

PITFALL

Some **geographical names** require the definite article as an inseparable part of the name while others stand alone. However, the article is often omitted by newscasters and in newspapers.

Typical examples

La Habana	Havana
El Brasil	Brazil
El Japón	Japan
El Canadá	Canada
La Florida	Florida
España	Spain
México	Mexico
Cuba	Cuba
Inglaterra	England
Suecia	Sweden

There is no rule about this; each must be remembered individually.

PITFALL

The definite article is required with all names of **countries** and **cities** when the place name is modified by an adjective or adjective phrase.

La España moderna
Modern Spain

El viejo Madrid de la verbena
Old Madrid of the street carnival

———————————— RULE ————————————

The definite article is used before units of **weight** or **measure** in Spanish where the indefinite article is required in English.

Spanish: **Estas naranjas cuestan 125 pesetas *el* kilo.**
English: These oranges cost 125 pesetas *a* kilo.

Spanish: **Recibimos un dólar *la* docena.**
English: We receive one dollar *a* dozen.

———————————— RULE ————————————

The definite article is used before the names of the **seasons** of the year, where it is not required in English.

Nos gusta nadar en el verano.
We like to swim in summer.

El invierno es la estación más triste del año.
Winter is the saddest season of the year.

En la primavera todo renace.
In springtime everything is reborn.

PITFALL

The definite article is often used in Spanish to refer back to a previously stated noun. (Also see section on Pronouns.)

Me gustan estos discos y *los* de María también.
I like these records and Mary's too. (Literally "the [ones] of Mary")

Mi coche es azul; *el* de mi hermana es rojo.
My car is blue; my sister's is red. (Literally "the [one] of my sister. . .")

------------------------------ RULE ------------------------------

In phrasing sentences that begin in English with expressions such as "We Americans. . . ," "You Spaniards. . . ," "We men. . . ," etc., the definite article is required between the pronoun and the noun.

English: We Spaniards are very proud.
Spanish: **Nosotros los españoles somos muy orgullosos.**

English: We women are made for compassion and care.
Spanish: **Nosotras las mujeres estamos hechas para la compasión y el cuidado.**
(In either of the above examples the pronoun *nosotros* (*as*) could be omitted without making the sentence incorrect.)

English: You children are the most innocent of all.
Spanish: **Vosotros los niños sois los más inocentes de todos.**

PITFALL

The definite article is omitted before a noun in apposition with another noun, except when a superlative is involved or an identification required.   EL
                                                    ^
Unamuno, autor de *Niebla* y *Abel Sánchez*, murió en 1936.
Unamuno, the author of *Niebla* and *Abel Sánchez,* died in 1936.

Nueva York, capital financiera de los Estados Unidos, es una ciudad de rascacielos.
New York, the financial capital of the United States, is a city of skyscrapers.

But:

Nueva York, la ciudad más grande de los Estados Unidos, es la capital financiera. *(Superlative)*
New York, the largest city in the United States, is the financial capital.

Chicago, la llamada segunda ciudad de los Estados Unidos, tiene más de tres millones de habitantes. *(Identification)*
Chicago, the so-called second city of the United States, has more than three million inhabitants.

THE INDEFINITE ARTICLE

Forms of the Indefinite Article

	Masculine	**Feminine**
Singular	un	una
Plural	unos	unas

un libro	**una lámpara**
unos libros	**unas lámparas**

PITFALL

The masculine article *un* is often used with singular feminine nouns beginning with a stressed *a* or *ha*.

un alma	a soul
un águila	an eagle
un hacha	an axe

OMISSION OF INDEFINITE ARTICLE IN SPANISH

PITFALL

Unlike English, Spanish omits the indefinite article with **unmodified**

nouns indicating nationality, profession, or affiliation when these
nouns occur in a predicate position, i.e., when they follow a verb and
do not initiate the action.

Unmodified:	**Mi hermano es médico.**
	My brother is a doctor.
	Soy estudiante; mi amigo es programador.
	I'm a student; my friend's a programmer.
Modified:	**Mi hermano es un médico famoso.** _modification_
	My brother is a famous doctor.
As a subject:	**Un médico llegó a las dos de la mañana.**
	A doctor arrived at two in the morning.

PITFALL

In expressions where the adjectives *bueno* and *malo* precede the
noun, the indefinite article may be omitted.

Hoy es buen día.
Today's a fine day.

María es buena persona.
Mary is a fine person.

—————————— RULE ——————————

The indefinite article is omitted before the words *ciento, mil, otro,
medio,* and *cierto* and after *tal* in the expression "such a" and *qué* in
the expression "what a."

cien pesos	a hundred pesos
cierto hombre	a certain man
mil habitantes	a thousand inhabitants
media docena	a half dozen
otra máquina	another machine
¡qué rica!	what a dear (girl)!
tal cosa	such a thing

PITFALL

The indefinite article is omitted after a preposition unless it carries the meaning of "one" to indicate number.

Ella viaja siempre sin bolsa.
She always travels without a purse.

Ella salió de Barajas con una maleta y dos bolsas.
She left Barajas (Madrid airport) with one suitcase and two purses.

THE NEUTER ARTICLE *LO*

──────────────── RULE ────────────────

Although neuter gender does not exist for nouns in Spanish, there is a neuter definite article (*lo*) as well as neuter demonstratives—which is used with a masculine singular adjective or with a past participle to form an abstract noun (that is, a noun that cannot refer to a specific person or thing, but which does express or sum up an idea).

lo bueno	the good part (thing)
lo triste	the sad part
lo perdido	the lost part, what is lost

──────────────── RULE ────────────────

Lo is also used before adjectives or adverbs to translate the English "how" when it expresses degree.

Se da cuenta de lo bonita que es Carmen.
He realizes how pretty Carmen is.

PITFALL

The expression *lo de* + **a noun, adverb, or infinitive** is frequently used in Spanish and has several possible English translations.

Lo de estudiar me cansa.
All this business about studying tires me.
(Literally: "The (business) of studying...")

En un televisor de color lo importante es lo de adentro.
In a color television the important part is what's inside.

PITFALL

Lo also occurs in many idiomatic expressions.

Lo Used in Idiomatic Expressions

a lo largo	along
a lo lejos	in the distance
a lo mejor	probably
a lo más	at most
a lo menos	at least
por lo general	generally
por lo pronto	for the time being
por lo tanto	consequently
por lo visto	apparently

Demonstrative Adjectives

A demonstrative adjective points out or fixes the word it modifies in place or time. The Spanish demonstratives are used like the comparable forms in English; however, Spanish demonstratives must agree in number and gender with the noun they modify. Spanish also differs from English in that it has two ways of saying **that** and **those**.

- this—**este, esta, estos, estas**
- that (nearby)—**ese, esa, esos, esas**
- that (at a distance or out of sight)—**aquel, aquella, aquellos, aquellas**

PITFALL

Do not confuse the masculine singular *este* and *ese* with the neuter demonstrative pronouns *esto* and *eso*.

	this record
INCORRECT SPANISH:	**esto disco**
CORRECT SPANISH:	*este disco*

	that friend of mine
INCORRECT SPANISH:	**eso amigo mío**
CORRECT SPANISH:	*ese amigo mío*

But the correct plural forms of the examples above would be: *estos discos* and *esos amigos míos.*

PITFALL

Although demonstratives usually precede the noun, occasionally they follow the word that is modified. In these instances there may be a derogatory implication or the suggestion of contempt.

La chica esa tiene dos novios.
That so-and-so (girl) has two boyfriends.

El tipo ese pasa todo el día en el bar.
That character spends the whole day in the bar.

Possessive Adjectives

Possessive adjectives indicate whether the owner or possessor of a noun is first person (my, our), second person (your), or third person (his, her, its, their, your). Spanish has two sets of possessives. *The short and more common forms* precede the noun; the *long forms* follow the noun and are more limited in their use. Unlike English, the Spanish possessive adjectives all agree in number (singular or plural) with the noun they modify, and those forms ending in *o* must also agree in gender (masculine or feminine) with the noun.

mi coche my car	**nuestro coche** our car
mis coches my cars	**nuestros coches** our cars
mi tía my aunt	**nuestra tía** our aunt
mis tías my aunts	**nuestras tías** our aunts

The Two Sets of Possessive Adjectives

Short Forms   **mi(s)**—my
tu(s)—your *(tú)*
su(s)—his, her, its, your *(usted)*
nuestro (a, os, as)—our
vuestro (a, os, as)—your *(vosotros)*
su(s)—their, your *(ustedes)*

Long Forms   **mío, mía, míos, mías**—my (of mine)
tuyo, tuya, tuyos, tuyas—your (of yours)
suyo, suya, suyos, suyas—his, her, its, your (of his, of hers, etc.)
nuestro (a, os, as)—our (of ours)
vuestro (a, os, as)—your (of yours)
suyo (a, os, as)—their, your (of theirs, of yours)

—————————— RULE ——————————

The long, stressed forms of the possessive adjective are used especially for emphasis, in direct address, after the verb *ser* (to be) to indicate simple possession, and for formation of possessive pronouns. (See section on pronouns.)

Emphasis:	**Ese chico no es amigo mío.**
	That boy isn't a friend of mine.
	(He's not *my* friend.)
Direct Address:	**Hijo mío, ¿qué buscas en la vida?**
	My boy, what are you seeking in life?

Simple	**Juan, estas llaves son tuyas.**
Possession	John, these keys are yours.
After *Ser:*	
	Señor, la culpa ha sido suya.
	Sir, you were to blame.
	(the blame has been yours)

PITFALL

English has three singular possessives to indicate third person and to distinguish between third person masculine, feminine, and neuter (his, her, its). Spanish, however, has a single form (*su*) which contains no indication of the gender of the possessor; the same form also serves for the third person plural (their). Spanish also indicates with the possessive adjective whether the thing possessed is singular or plural, while the English forms show no indication of number.

For example:

su deseo might mean any of the following in English:

his wish (desire)	your wish
her wish	their wish
its wish	

And *sus deseos* has an equal number of possible meanings:

his wishes	your wishes
her wishes	their wishes
its wishes	

In short, *su* and *sus* simply indicate any third-person possession in Spanish; however, the situation in which the adjective and noun occur generally gives us a clue as to *which* third person is involved. Where there is a chance of doubt or ambiguity, there are simple means of clarification. For example:

Jorge me dio *su* llave.
George gave me *his* key.

Normally we would suppose that *su* means "his" in this sentence, or some preceding or following statement would indicate the correct ownership. However, if clarification is required, the sentence could be expressed:

> **Jorge me dio la llave de él.**
> or
> **Jorge me dio su llave de él.**

Similarly, *la (su) llave de ella* would mean "her key," *la llave de usted (es)* would mean "your key" and *la llave de ellos (as)* "their key."

Note that "its key," meaning *"la llave de la puerta"* or *"la llave del apartamento,"* would be:

> **la llave de ella (la puerta)**
> or
> **la llave de él (el apartamento)**

PITFALL

There is no neuter word for "it" in Spanish when referring to things. Unlike English, masculine and feminine genders do not necessarily have any relationship to sex (male or female).

> **¿Tienes la llave para *la puerta?***
> **¿Tienes la llave para ella?**
> Do you have the key for it?

PITFALL

It would be repetitious and incorrect to try to clarify the possessives *mi, tu, nuestro,* and *vuestro* since the possessor intended is unmistakable.

INCORRECT: **la (tu) llave de ti**

                    la (nuestra) llave de nosotros

CORRECT: *tu llave*   your key

                   nuestra llave   our key

PITFALL

The definite article *(el, la, los, las)* often replaces the possessive adjective when parts of the body or personal possessions such as clothing are involved.

Tiene *los* zapatos en *la* mano.

He has his shoes in his hand.

Nos quitamos *el* sombrero.

We take off our hats.

(not *los sombreros,* since each person removes a single hat.)

PITFALL

Frequently the possessor is indicated by a reflexive pronoun (see example above) or by an indirect object pronoun. Compare the English and Spanish word order in these cases.

English: *Your fever has gone down.*

          Poss.Adj.   Noun   Verb

Spanish: *Te ha bajado la fiebre.*

          Ind.Obj.   Verb   Noun & Article
          Pronoun

Indefinite and Negative Adjectives

The adjective *alguno* (some) cannot describe or define a person or thing; the negative form *ninguno* serves to point out the nonexistence of a person or thing. Both show agreement with the nouns they modify, and both drop the final *o* before a masculine singular noun.

Ningún hombre haría eso.
No man would do that.

Algunos estudiantes asisten a una clase especial.
Some students are attending a special class.

No hay ninguna aeromoza (azafata) en el avión.
There is no flight attendant on the plane.
(There's not a single one aboard.)

Alguno and *ninguno* occur in many frequently used expressions. Some of the most common are:

algún día	someday
alguna vez	sometime
de alguna manera	in some way
de algún modo	in some way
de ninguna manera	in no way
de ningún modo	in no way, by no means
en ninguna parte	nowhere

PITFALL

Alguno normally precedes its noun but it may follow and acquire a meaning of emphatic negation.

Este programa no tiene interés alguno.
This program has no interest at all.

PITFALL

Varios may also be used to mean "some" and is always plural. It may contain the idea of "various."

Aquí se venden varios libros sobre la filosofía.
Various (some) books on philosophy are for sale here.

Interrogative Adjectives

The common interrogative adjectives are *¿qué . . . ?* (what, which?) and *¿cuánto. . .?* (how much [many]?).

¿Qué disco prefiere usted?
Which disc do you prefer?

¿Cuánta pobreza se puede soportar?
How much poverty can one endure?

PITFALL

In exclamations *¡qué . . .!* may have the meaning of "what a!" and "how. . . !"

¡Qué bonito!	How pretty!
¡Qué vino magnífico!	What a superb wine!

PITFALL

At times *tan* or *más* is used to intensify exclamations. Note the difference between Spanish and English word order. Once more it can be seen that literal translations can lead to errors in expression.

English: What a very   amusing film!
                        "terribly"

Spanish: **¿Qué película tan divertida!**
                                más

PITFALL

In colloquial speech *¿cuál . . . ?* is sometimes used in place of *¿qué . . . ?*; however, in the strictest sense, *cuál* is a pronoun and should not be used as an adjective.

English: Which book do you prefer?

Colloquial: **¿Cuál libro prefieres?**

CORRECT: *¿Qué libro prefieres?*
                   (or *¿Cuál de los libros prefieres?*)

Numerals

Numbers—both cardinal *(uno, dos, tres,* etc.) and ordinal *(primero, segundo, tercero,* etc.)—function as adjectives. (See also section on Measurements.)

trece páginas	thirteen pages
el tercer acto	the third act
or	
el acto tercero	

The ordinals above *décimo* (tenth) are rarely used. Normally the cardinal numbers take over at this point.

la quinta generación	the fifth generation
el piso veinte	the twentieth floor

─────────────── RULE ───────────────

Ordinals may precede or follow the noun they modify. When they follow, they distinguish a person or thing from another. Most commonly this occurs with names of royalty, or with chapters of books and acts of plays.

Felipe Segundo	Philip the Second
Acto Segundo	Act Two

PITFALL

Note that Spanish does not use the article "the" in royal titles.

Carlos Quinto (Carlos V)	Charles the Fifth (Charles V)

——————————— RULE ———————————

The cardinal number *ciento* (one hundred) drops the final *to* before all nouns, and before *mil* and *millón*; the ordinals *primero* and *tercero* drop the final *o* when they precede a masculine singular noun. (See also section on Shortened Adjectives.)

cien mil dólares	a hundred thousand dollars
cien páginas	a hundred pages
el Primer Ministro	the Prime (first) Minister

PITFALL

Unlike English, neither *mil* or *cien (to)* requires the article or determiner, *un.*

English:	one (a) thousand kilometers
Spanish:	**mil kilómetros**

PITFALL

Millón is a noun and not an adjective; consequently it must be followed by the preposition *de* whenever it is used with another noun.

English:	five million pesetas
Spanish:	**cinco millones de pesetas**

PITFALL

Unlike English, whenever *primero* and a cardinal number modify the same noun, the cardinal number comes first.

English:	the first three chapters
Spanish:	**los tres primeros capítulos**

PITFALL

Spanish also has a reverse order from English when *otro* and a cardinal number modify a noun.

English: two other candidates
Spanish: **otros dos candidatos**

SPECIAL USES
Shortened Adjectives—Apocopation

──────────────── RULE ────────────────

A number of Spanish adjectives, all of which may occur before or after the noun, drop the ending *o* when they precede a masculine noun: *bueno, malo, primero, tercero, alguno, ninguno.*

el *primer* piso	but	el piso *primero*
		la *primera* casa
el *buen* señor	but	el señor *bueno*
		los *buenos* señores
ningún hombre	but	hombre *ninguno*

──────────────── RULE ────────────────

Grande The adjective *grande* drops the final *de* before any singular noun. In the plural it retains its complete form.

la gran actriz	but	las grandes actrices
un gran presidente	&middot;	los grandes presidentes

──────────────── RULE ────────────────

Santo Santo, which translates the English "saint" as well as meaning "holy," drops the final *to* when followed by any masculine name except *Domingo* and *Tomás.*

San Pedro	but	**Santo Tomás**
(Saint Peter)		(Saint Thomas)
San Juan		
(Saint John)		

PITFALL

Note, however, that *santa* is always the feminine form.

Santa Ana
(Saint Anne)

Semana Santa
(Holy Week)

─────────────── RULE ───────────────

Ciento The number *ciento* (one hundred) is shortened to *cien* before all nouns, which include *millón* (million), and before *mil* (thousand).

cien aviones   but   **trescientos aviones**
(a hundred airplanes)   (three hundred airplanes)

cien mil estudiantes
(a hundred thousand students)

cien millones de pesetas
(a hundred million pesetas)

Participles as Adjectives

─────────────── RULE ───────────────

As in English, the **past participle** (*hablado*—spoken, *callado*—hushed, *sentido*—felt) may be used as an adjective in Spanish. This participial adjective must also show agreement with the noun it modifies.

Es un hombre de avanzada edad.
He's a man of advanced age.

El payaso gritó: "Distinguido público!"
The clown shouted: "Distinguished public!"

29

PITFALL

At times the Spanish **past participle** may require an English present participle for translation.

Spanish: **La señora sentada en el coche es su secretaria.**

English: The lady sitting (seated) in the car is his secretary.

PITFALL

Unlike English, the Spanish **present participle** (called the *gerundio* but not equivalent to the English gerund) may not be used in an adjective sense. But there exist in Spanish adjectives of participial origin, ending in -*ante* or -*iente*, which may modify nouns and which are not used as verbs. (For further discussion of Present Participles see section on Verbs.)

En la **ardiente** *oscuridad* **es un drama de Buero Vallejo.**
In the Burning *Darkness* is a drama by Buero Vallejo.

Escriba las frases *siguientes* **(not** *siguiendo*)
Write the *following* sentences.

Adjectives Used as Nouns—Nominalization

———————————— RULE ————————————

Adjectives frequently assume the quality of nouns when the accompanying noun is omitted or dropped.

El rojo **me gusta más que** *el verde.*
(Speaking of *un suéter* or some other masculine sing. noun.)
I like the red (one) more than the green (one).

Esa *joven* **parece muy triste.**
(Refers to *señorita* or *muchacha.*)
That young person (girl) seems very sad.

PITFALL

Spanish nouns cannot be used as adjectives—as often occurs in English.

English:	a brick house
Spanish:	**una casa de ladrillos**
	(literally: a house of bricks)

English:	a silver bracelet
Spanish:	**una pulsera de plata**
	(literally: a bracelet of silver)

English:	a Spanish professor
Spanish:	**un profesor de español**
	(by profession, but without implying Spanish birth)

Special Adjectives

PITFALL Cada

Cada (each, every) has a single, invariable form regardless of what follows.

cada persona	each person
cada libro	each book
(not *cado* **libro**)	

In a plural situation *cada* is usually accompanied by a number.

cada tres días	every three days

To express the English "every other," *cada dos* is used rather than *"cada otro."*

English:	every other line
INCORRECT:	**cada otra línea**
CORRECT:	*cada dos líneas*

PITFALL Todo

The English "every," when referring to a class or category, is expressed in Spanish by **todo** (*a*).

> **Toda mujer debe tener derechos políticos.**
> Every woman should have political rights.

Todos in the plural,translating the English "all (of)" or "every," is followed directly by the article and the noun without the preposition *de* (of)—which is frequently incorrectly inserted by the English-speaking student

> **todos los días**
> every day
>
> **todos los años**
> every year, all years
>
> **Todas las manzanas son rojísimas.**
> All (of) the apples are very red.

PITFALL Demás

Demás ([the] rest of [the]) is an unchangeable adjective. The same form is always used regardless of the gender of the noun that follows.

> **Las demás monedas valen muy poco.**
> The rest of the coins are worth very little.
>
> **Los demás cheques son para usted.**
> The rest of the checks are for you.

PITFALL Ambos

Ambos (both) is by nature of its meaning always plural. *Los dos* has the same meaning. Note that the article *(los, las)* should not be used with *ambos*.

English:	Both doctors are specialists.
Spanish:	**Ambos médicos son especialistas.**

or

Los dos médicos son especialistas.

COMPARISON OF ADJECTIVES

A person or thing may be compared with another person or thing in terms of a certain quality to show superiority, inferiority, or equality: "My mother is younger than my father," or "George is more likeable than his friends," or "I am as ambitious as my brother." In English the comparative of the adjective is formed by adding "-er" to the adjective or by using "more," "less," or "as" with the adjective. In Spanish only a limited number of adjectives have a true comparative form:

bueno (good)	**mejor** (better)
malo (bad)	**peor** (worse)
grande (large)	**mayor** (larger, older)
	(also **más grande** when referring to size)
pequeño (small)	**menor** (smaller, younger)
	(also **más pequeño** when referring to size)
mucho (much, many)	**más** (more)
poco (little)	**menos** (less)

PITFALL

With other adjectives the comparative is formed with *más* or *menos*. The English "than" is translated by *que* in Spanish except before a number, in which case *de* is required.

Esta telecomedia es más interesante que las otras.
This television play is more interesting than the others.

But:

Tengo más de treinta libros raros.
I have more than thirty rare books.

PITFALL

Although comparatives may precede or follow the noun, *menor* and *mayor* usually follow.

el hermano mayor
the older (*or* oldest) brother

la hermana menor
the younger (*or* youngest) sister

PITFALL

Grande and *pequeño* are sometimes compared regularly but only when referring to size rather than age.

El VW Golf es más pequeño que el modelo nuevo.
The VW Golf (car) is smaller than the new model.

PITFALL

Bueno and *malo* may also be compared regularly when referring to character traits. Otherwise *mejor* and *peor* are required.

La señora Ortiz es más buena que sus vecinos.
Mrs. Ortiz is better (a better person) than her neighbors.
But:
Esta aspirina es mejor que ésas.
This aspirin is better than those.

PITFALL

In comparisons of equality, the Spanish **tan + adjective** and **como + noun** are equivalent to the English formulas: **as + adjective** and **as + noun**.

English: George is as tall as his father.
Spanish: **Jorge es tan alto como su padre.**

PITFALL

The Spanish **tanto + noun + como** translates the English formula: **as much + noun + as.** A literal translation of English results in an incorrect statement.

English:	He has as much money as I (have).
INCORRECT SPANISH:	**Tiene tan mucho dinero como yo.**
CORRECT SPANISH:	*Tiene tanto dinero como yo.*

SUPERLATIVES

——————————— RULE ———————————

To form a superlative—indicating that a person or thing possesses a quality to a higher degree than all others—the definite article (*el, la, los, las*) is added to the comparative form of the Spanish adjective (*el más fuerte*—the strongest, *la peor*—the worst, etc.).

El SEAT Ibiza es el coche más cómodo.
The SEAT Ibiza is the most comfortable car.

María es la más feliz.
Mary is the happiest (one).

Tony es el menos listo de los tres hermanos.
Tony is the least clever of the three brothers.

——————————— RULE ———————————

When a prepositional phrase follows the superlative, *de* is required in Spanish where "in" is correct in English.

Fabricantes de las impresoras más solicitadas *del* mundo.
Makers of the most sought after printers *in* the world.

Es el mejor matemático *de* la universidad.
He's the best mathematician *in* the university.
(*Or*: He's the university's best mathematician.)

Absolute Superlatives— *-ísimo, -ísima*

Spanish also has a form of the adjective known as "the absolute superlative" which indicates that a person or thing possesses a quality to an unusual or exceeding degree; however, it is not used to compare a person or thing with someone or something else. It is formed by adding *-ísimo (-a)* to adjectives that end in a consonant *(dificilísimo)*; adjectives that end in a vowel drop the final vowel before adding *-ísimo (rojísimo)*. Frequently, more than one English translation is possible for the Spanish absolute superlative.

Spanish:	**Este problema es facilísimo.**	
English:	This problem is	very easy.
		exceedingly easy.
		extraordinarily easy.
		etc.

PITFALL

Spanish may also use other constructions to convey a degree more or less comparable to that indicated by the ending *-ísimo.*

> **Este problema es muy fácil.**
> or
> **Este problema es sumamente fácil.**

PITFALL

A spelling change is required when forming the absolute superlative of adjectives ending in *co* or *go*:

simpático, -a	**simpatiquísimo, -a**
amargo, -a	**amarguísimo, -a**

This is not an irregularity—rather it is in keeping with the requirement of Spanish that words be spelled the way they are pronounced. (Also see section on Pronunciation.)

2 Adverbs

THE USE OF ADVERBS

Adverbs may be single words, phrases, or clauses (see section on Verbs for presentation of Adverbial Clauses). They have the same relation to verbs that adjectives have to nouns, defining or qualifying the action of a verb or limiting the action of a verb in time or space. Adverbs may also modify an adjective or a participle (*muy bonito, muy avanzada*). Unlike adjectives, the form of an adverb can show no type of agreement with the word it modifies.

Use of the Suffix -*mente*

In addition to those words whose single function is adverbial *(anteayer, aquí, tampoco, etc.)*, adverbs can be formed by adding the suffix -*mente* to the feminine singular form of adjectives that end in *o*, or to the invariable singular form of other adjectives (*claramente, atrozmente, fácilmente, etc.*).

PITFALL

If two (or more) adverbs ending in -*mente* occur in sequence, only the last one carries the suffix.

> **Juan habló tranquila y pausadamente.**
> John spoke calmly and deliberately.

PITFALL

More often than in English we find in Spanish a prepositional phrase—*con* **+ an abstract noun**—substituted for the -*mente* (or -ly) form of the adverb.

> **con ironía** for **irónicamente**
> (ironically)
>
> **con cuidado** for **cuidadosamente**
> (carefully)

As in the case of the second example, the prepositional phrase may be easier to say or may appear less cumbersome than the longer form ending in -*mente*. Other prepositional phrases are also commonly used in an adverbial sense, but the preposition(s) in the phrase should not be expected to correspond to the one(s) used in similar English expressions.

de noche	at night, by night (not **anoche**, which means "last night" in Spanish)
de día	by day
de vez en cuando	from time to time
a lo lejos	in the distance
a la francesa	(in the) French style
a ciegas	blindly

PITFALL

Adverbs formed from adjectives that carry a written accent to indicate the stressed syllable retain the accent even though the principal stress falls on the adverbial ending -*mente*.

Adjective	Adverb
rápido	**rápidamente**
fácil	**fácilmente**

PITFALL

The adverb *recientemente* is shortened to *recién* before a past participle.

Son inmigrantes recién llegados.
They are recently arrived immigrants.

PITFALL

In addition to the adverbs **sólo** and **solamente**, the phrase **no más que** exists as a translation of the English adverb "only."

Tiene sólo cincuenta pesetas.
(solamente)
He has only fifty pesetas.
or
No tiene más que cincuenta pesetas.
He has only fifty pesetas (that is, "no more than fifty").

TYPES OF ADVERBS

Sometimes the meaning of an adjective excludes its use as an adverb in ordinary expression even though the adverbial form might theoretically exist. [For example, adverbs based on adjectives such as *mundial* (world-wide), *aéreo* (air, by air), and rubio (blond, light-haired) or certain past participles used as adjectives—*arrugado* (wrinkled), *perdido* (lost)—would not be expected.] For a clearer understanding of adverbs it is helpful to group them in different categories.

Type of Adverb	Typical Examples
Place	**aquí, acá** (here), **ahí, allí, allá,** (there), **dentro** (within, inside), **fuera** (outside), **abajo** (below, downstairs), **arriba** (above, upstairs), **encima** (on top), **cerca** (near), **lejos** (far)
Time	**hoy** (today), **mañana** (tomorrow), **ayer** (yesterday), **anteayer** (the day before yesterday), **temprano** (early), **tarde** (late), **nunca** (never), **siempre** (always), **ahora** (now), **luego** (then)

Manner	**como** (how), **bien** (well), **mal** (poorly, badly), **despacio** (slowly), **apenas** (scarcely), and many others ending in **-mente**
Quantity	**muy** (**mucho**) (very, a lot), **poco** (little), **bastante** (enough, rather), **tan, tanto** (so, so much), **más** (more)
Negation	**no** (no, not), **tampoco** (either, neither) **nunca** (never), **nada** (not at all)
Order	**antes** (before), **después** (afterwards) **primero** (first)
Doubt	**acaso, quizás, tal vez** (perhaps)
Affirmation	**sí** (yes), **cómo no** (why not), **por supuesto** (of course)
Concession	**sin embargo** (nevertheless)

PITFALL

Algo is sometimes used in an adverbial sense to mean "rather." It should not be confused with *algo* used as a pronoun.

As an adverb:	**Ese examen fue algo difícil.**
	That examination was rather (*or* somewhat) difficult.
As a pronoun:	**Has dicho algo que no entiendo.**
	You've said something that I don't understand.

PITFALL

A common way of expressing manner is with the expressions *de una manera* (or *de manera)* and *de un modo (*or *de modo)* plus an adjective.

Cantaban de una manera feliz.
They were singing happily. (in a happy way)

PITFALL

As in English, some adverbs function as interrogative words or to introduce an exclamatory sentence.

¿*Cómo* se llama?
What's your name?
(Literally: "How do you call yourself?")

¿*Dónde* encontró el tesoro?
Where did he find the treasure?

¡*Cuánto* te quiero!
How (much) I love you!

¡*Qué* linda es tu hermana!
How pretty your sister is!

(Note the difference between Spanish and English word order here.)

PITFALL

The English **"how" + an adverb** in a non-exclamatory sentence is not translated by *como,* but by the neuter article **lo + an adverb + que**.

English: He realized *how well* they were playing.
Spanish: **Se dio cuenta de *lo bien que* tocaban.**

Note that an equivalent of the Spanish *que* is not required in the English sentence.

POSITION OF ADVERBS

There are no absolute rules for the placement of adverbs in a sentence, but very frequently the adverb will be placed immediately following the verb it modifies; it normally comes immediately before an adjective or another adverb that is modified.

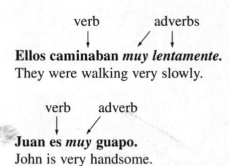

verb   adverbs

Ellos caminaban *muy lentamente*.
They were walking very slowly.

verb   adverb

Juan es *muy* guapo.
John is very handsome.

There are, of course, many exceptions in the placement of adverb and verb. Adverbs consisting of two or more words usually come last in a sentence or clause.

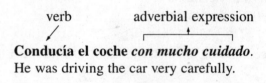

verb   adverbial expression

Conducía el coche *con mucho cuidado*.
He was driving the car very carefully.

─────────────── RULE ───────────────
For emphasis, adverbs may be placed at the beginning of a sentence.
───────────────────────────────────

adverb   verb

***Aquí* se venden todos los libros más recientes.**
All the most recent books are sold here.

PITFALL

In an expression in which *no* and an adverb stand alone, Spanish usage is the reverse of English; that is, *no* (not) follows the adverb.

Todavía no.   **Mañana no.**
Not yet.   Not tomorrow.

PITFALL

Adverbs never separate the two parts of a compound tense as they often do in English.

Siempre me ha gustado viajar.
I have *always* liked to travel.

PITFALL

Occasionally an adjective is employed after a verb in Spanish where English would normally require an adverb. This should not be confused with the frequent misuse of adjectives as adverbs in colloquial English.

CORRECT SPANISH: **Las chicas entraron ruidosas.**
(That is, "The girls were noisy when they came in.")

CORRECT ENGLISH: The girls came in noisily.

INCORRECT ENGLISH: The girls came in noisy.

COMPARISON OF ADVERBS

Adverbs are compared like adjectives (i.e., by placing *más* or *menos* before the adverb). Only four adverbs have irregular comparative forms.

mucho	alot, very	**más**	more
poco	little	**menos**	less
bien	well	**mejor**	better
mal	badly	**peor**	worse

Este estudiante habla mejor que yo.
This student speaks better than I.

Carmen trabaja menos que la otra secretaria.
Carmen works less than the other secretary.

..quel país los ministros cambian más rápidamente que las estaciones.
In that country the officials (ministers) change more rapidly than the seasons.

PITFALL

In comparisons of equality, the English formula "**as + adverb + as**" is translated into Spanish by "***tan + adverb + como***."

Ella no habla tan claramente como él.
She doesn't speak as clearly as he.

PITFALL

To express the adverbial phrase "as much as," Spanish uses the invariable *tanto como*.

Nadie sufre tanto como esa señora.
No one suffers as much as that lady.

PITFALL

The Spanish *que* normally translates the English "than" when two things, persons, or actions are compared; however, before numbers *de* is used instead of *que* to translate "than."

Este semestre estudiamos más que antes.
This semester we are studying more than before.

Esta mañana me quedan menos de cinco duros.
This morning I have less than five *duros* left.
(un duro = cinco pesetas)

PITFALL

When entire ideas are compared, *de lo que* is required where the single English word "than" suffices.

Este señor trabaja más *de lo que* ustedes piensan.
This gentleman works more *than* you think.

("This gentleman works" represents the first idea, and "you think" is the second idea.)

PITFALL

An adverbial superlative may be expressed by the neuter **article *lo* +** *más* (or *menos*) + **adverb** + *posible*.

Espero que me devuelvas el libro lo más pronto posible.
I hope that you'll return the book to me as soon as possible.

POTENTIAL PITFALLS WITH ADVERBS
Here and *There*

The demonstrative adverbs *aquí* and *acá* (both meaning "here"), and *allí, ahí, allá* (all meaning "there"), cannot be used interchangeably.

PITFALL

Aquí refers to a place or location near the speaker and should not be used with a verb of motion.

Aquí se venden discos.
Records are sold here.

PITFALL

Acá, also referring to the vicinity of the speaker, is used with verbs of motion (that is, when movement from one place to another closer to the speaker is indicated).

Paco, ven acá.
Paco, come here.

PITFALL

Ahí refers to a place relatively close to the speaker or subject.

Ponga usted las maletas ahí.
Put the suitcases there.

PITFALL

Allí indicates a determined location far or remote from the speaker. (The difference between *ahí* and *allí* is similar to that which exists between the demonstrative adjectives *ese* and *aquel,* and the pronoun forms *ése* and *aquél.*)

Oaxaca está en el sur de México. Mi primo vive allí.
Oaxaca is in the south of Mexico. My cousin lives there.

PITFALL

Allá, like *acá,* is usually used with verbs of motion, or to express a vagueness about a distant location.

Quisiera ir allá, donde la vida es mejor.
I'd like to go there, where life is better.

PITFALL

The expression *el más allá* is equivalent to the English "the great beyond" or "the other world."

Quizás nos veamos en el más allá.
Perhaps we'll see each other in the other world.

Muy and Mucho

PITFALL

Muy is the adverbial form of the adjective *mucho.* However, in a comparative sentence *mucho* serves as the adverb. Note that *mucho,* being used as an adverb, cannot show any agreement with the adjective it modifies.

Estos son mucho mejores que los otros.
These are much better than the others.

El lo hizo mucho mejor de lo que creíamos.
He did it much better than we believed.

PITFALL

Muy is not used alone. When an English sentence calls for the simple word "very," it becomes *mucho*.

¿Es bonita su novia? Sí, *mucho*.
Is his girlfriend pretty? Yes, very.

PITFALL

A literal translation of the English "so much" is impossible in Spanish. *Tan mucho,* a nonexistent form, is *not* an acceptable substitute for *tanto*.

English: They have so much money!
Spanish: **¡Tienen tanto dinero!** (not **tan mucho dinero**)

English: These children talk so much!
Spanish: **¡Estos chicos hablan tanto!** (not **tan mucho**)

PITFALL

When an adjective is modified, *tan* (so) and not *tanto* is the required form.

¡Es tan largo el camino!
The road is so long!

PITFALL

The adverbs *bastante* (enough) and *demasiado* (too much) are occasionally used as adjectives and then show the same type of agreement as other adjectives.

As adverbs:	**¿Quieres otra tortilla? No, he comido bastante.** Do you want another tortilla? No, I've eaten enough. **He bebido demasiado.** I've drunk too much.
As adjectives:	**No hay bastantes libros para los estudiantes.** There aren't enough books for the students. **Hay demasiados ladrones en este barrio.** There are too many thieves in this neighborhood.

THE VERB *TENER*

PITFALL

For beginning language students an especially troublesome difference between English and Spanish is the use of *tener* (to have) as the basic verb in certain expressions that require the verb "to be" in English.

The basic English formula is: subject + appropriate form of "to be" + adjective (or adverb & adjective).

The basic Spanish formula is: subject + appropriate form of *tener* + noun (or adjective & noun).

adv. adj.
↓   ↓

English: I am very cold.

adj. noun
↓   ↓

Spanish: **Tengo mucho frío.** (Literally: I have much cold[ness].)

adv. adj.
↓   ↓

English: You ought to be very ashamed.

	adj. noun

Spanish: **Debieras tener mucha vergüenza.**
(Literally: You ought to have much shame.)

adv.

English: I wasn't very hungry but I had lunch with her.

adj.

Spanish: **No tenía mucha hambre, pero almorcé con ella.**

3 Conjunctions

A conjunction is a linking word (or combination of words) that may join single words, groups of words, or complete ideas expressed in two or more clauses.

Pedro _y_ Carlos	Peter _and_ Charles
libros _y_ revistas	books _and_ magazines
listo _pero_ perezoso	clever _but_ lazy
en la cocina _o_ en el comedor	in the kitchen _or_ in the dining room
Ella escribió la novela en Chile _pero_ se publicó en México	She wrote the novel in Chile _but_ it was published in Mexico.

TYPES OF CONJUNCTIONS

There are three basic types of conjunctions: **coordinate, subordinate,** and **correlative.**

COORDINATE CONJUNCTIONS

Coordinate conjunctions are those that connect words, phrases, or clauses of the same kind. The common Spanish conjunctions of this type are _o_ (or), _ni_ (nor), _y_ (and), _pero_ (but), and _sino_ (but).

─────────────────── RULE ───────────────────

Before words beginning with _i_ or _hi_, the conjunction _y_ becomes _e_. (This prevents the combining of _y_ and _i_ into a single sound.)

Fernando *e* Isabel (not **Fernando y Isabel**)
Ferdinand *and* Isabella

aguja *e* hilo
needle *and* thread

PITFALL

This change does not occur, however, when *y* precedes *h* + the diphthong *ie*.

Aquí se encuentran cobre *y* hierro.
Copper and iron are found here.

───────────── RULE: ─────────────
Before a word beginning with *o* or *ho*, the conjunction *o* becomes *u*.

palabras *u* oraciones	words *or* sentences
mujeres *u* hombres	women *or* men

PITFALL

Although *pero* and *sino* both mean "but," *sino* may be used only when the first part of the sentence is negative and the second part contradicts the first part. *Sino que* and not *sino* alone is required when a clause is introduced.

Es muy viejo *pero* lo recuerda todo.
He is very old but he remembers it all.
(Two complete and non-contradictory ideas)

***El sueño de la razón* no es un drama de Sastre *sino* de Buero Vallejo.**
The Sleep of Reason is not a drama by Sastre but by Buero Vallejo.
(The second part of the sentence contradicts or corrects the *first* part.)

Un arquitecto pretendía derribar una basílica del siglo X y no restaurarla, *sino* **hacerla de nuevo como debía haber sido hecha.**

An architect aspired to tear down a basilica of the tenth century, and not to restore it but to rebuild it as it should have been built.

(Here *sino* has the meaning of "but rather." *Sino que* is not required because *hacerla* is not a conjugated form of the verb.)

No vendió el cuadro, *sino que* **se lo dio a un amigo.**

He didn't sell the picture but gave it to a friend. (*Sino que* is required because a clause is introduced.)

PITFALL

In literature, particularly poetry and drama written in verse, *mas* (but) is sometimes used instead of *pero*. This form is easily distinguishable from the adverb *más* because it does not carry an accent.

Ay, todavía
delante de mí le tengo. . .
Mas no existe, es ilusión
que imagina mi deseo.
                    ***(El trovador,* García Gutiérrez)**

Oh, I still have him before me. . .
But he does not exist, it is an
illusion that my desire creates (imagines).

Los ruiseñores se van; mas vuelven en primavera a cantar. . .
The nightingales depart; but they come back to sing again in the spring.

SUBORDINATE CONJUNCTIONS

A **subordinate conjunction** introduces a subordinate clause, i.e., a group of words containing a subject and verb but dependent on a main clause. (For a presentation of the subjunctive in subordinate clauses, see section on Verbs.)

Common Spanish Subordinate Conjunctions

a fin de que	in order that, so that
a menos que	unless
antes (de) que	before
así que	so that
aunque	although
como	as, since
como si	as if
con tal que	provided that
cuando	when
de modo que	so that
desde que	since
después (de) que	after
donde	where
en caso (de) que	in case
hasta que	until
mientras (que)	while
para que	in order that
porque	because
puesto que	since
que	that, for, because
si	if, whether
sin que	without

──────────────── RULE ────────────────

Only a conjunction or a relative pronoun can introduce a subordinate clause. Since a single English word may sometimes serve as an adverb, a preposition, and a conjunction in different situations where three distinct forms are required in Spanish, care must be exercised not to substitute an adverb or preposition where a conjunction is mandatory. (A conjunction must be used when a subject and verb follow the main clause.)

	Adverb	Preposition	Conjunction
English:	before	before	before
Spanish:	**antes**	**antes de**	**antes que**

INCORRECT:	**Ellos llegaron antes saliésemos.**
CORRECT:	*Ellos llegaron antes que saliésemos.*
	They arrived before we left.

INCORRECT:	**Suele salir sin nosotros lo oigamos.**
CORRECT:	*Suele salir sin que nosotros lo oigamos.*
	He usually leaves without our hearing him.
	(Literally: "without that we hear him.")

INCORRECT:	**Nos reímos después nos dio las buenas noticias.**
CORRECT:	*Nos reímos después que nos dio las buenas noticias.*
	We laughed after he gave us the good news.

PITFALL

The conjunction *que* most frequently translates the English "that," but occasionally it means "for" or "because," or simply does not exist in the English expression.

Dudo *que* llegues a tiempo.
I doubt *that* you'll arrive on time.

No te pongas insinuante con esa señora, *que* te conozco bien.
Don't get familiar with that lady, because I know you (too) well.

CORRELATIVE CONJUNCTIONS

Correlative conjunctions are used in pairs with intervening words.

Common Spanish Correlative Conjunctions

apenas . . . cuando	scarcely . . . when
ni . . . ni	neither . . . nor
o . . . o	either . . . or

Apenas nos saludó, cuando tuvimos que salir.
He'd scarcely greeted us when we had to leave.

Ni Juan ni su padre lo supieron hasta ayer.
Neither John nor his father found it out until yesterday.

O me dices la verdad o vas a sentirlo.
Either you tell me the truth or you're going to regret it.

PITFALL

When singular nouns (or pronouns) joined by *ni* or *o* precede the verb, the verb is usually plural. However, if the nouns (or pronouns) follow the verb, it is singular if only singular words are involved.

Lo curioso es que ni ella ni él lo saben.
The curious thing is that neither she nor he knows it

But:

No lo sabe ni Juan ni María
Neither John nor Mary knows it.

4 Interjections

EXCLAMATORY WORDS AND PHRASES

An **interjection** is an exclamatory word or expression that is uttered or written without any precise grammatical connection to sentences that precede or follow. (English: Oh!, Alas!, Gosh!, Bah!). (Spanish: *¡ay!, ¡toma!, ¡vaya!, ¡atiza!).* At times these are one syllable words whose spelling is an attempt to reproduce a mere cry or sound indicating some emotional reaction. (English: Ugh! Whew! Shhh!) (Spanish: *¡huy!, ¡zas!, ¡uf!, ¡je!, ¡chist!).*

PITFALL

Sometimes exclamations consist of a combination of words, and an entire sentence can, of course, be an exclamation.

English:	My goodness! How awful! Thank Heaven! How beautiful it is!
Spanish:	**¡Qué barbaridad!, ¡Qué raro!, ¡Qué bonito es!**

Other words closely akin to the exclamatory words are "filler" words that serve to fill up pauses between phrases and sentences or to preface a statement These are common in the spoken language but are rarely encountered in written form except in the dialogue of novels and plays. (English: er, well, why, etc.) (Spanish: *Pues, ya,* etc.).

The choice of exclamations may be influenced by the age, sex, education, social background, and emotional state of the speaker. Exclamations include many expressions that would be considered offensive to one group or another, and much caution must be exercised in using Spanish interjections and exclamations without previous first-hand experience with the language. Some words or phrases that may seem innocent enough in a literal translation have a suggested meaning that can be highly insulting. Also, certain words that are perfectly acceptable in one Spanish-speaking country may be taboo in another.

Several Spanish expletives begin with *ca*. These range from mild to explosive (*¡ca!, ¡caramba!, ¡caray!,* and others of increasing force).

RULE

Numerous exclamatory phrases are composed of **qué + a noun, verb, or adjective**, most frequently with the meaning of "what a. . . !" *Vaya* is also used with a noun with the English meaning "what a. . . !"

Combinations with *Qué* and *Vaya*

¡Qué fastidio!	What a nuisance!
¡Qué barbaridad!	How awful! (What a barbarity!)
¡Qué tío!	What a guy!
¡Vaya un chico!	What a boy!
¡Vaya (un) día!	What a day!
¡Vaya una cosa!	What are you saying!
	(Literally: What a thing!)

PITFALL

Exclamations and interjections are frequently untranslatable. But if a translation is called for, it is necessary to seek an "equivalent" that fits into the context of the sentence or passage involved. For example, the common Spanish exclamation *¡menos mal!* might mean:

> Things could be worse!
> Thank goodness for that!
> Thank Heaven for small blessings!
> So much the better!
> (and other similar exclamations of relief)

And the frequently used exclamations *¡vamos!* and *¡vaya!* (both are forms of the verb *ir*) could mean:

Well now!	Come on!
Well!	Go on!
Come now!	

And the similar exclamation *¡anda!* (from the verb *andar*) could have a similar list of meanings.

PITFALL

The use of religious names and name of the Deity in simple exclamations is not normally considered sacrilegious or offensive in Spanish unless these are employed in a violent or angry manner. Ordinary Spanish speech is filled with such expressions as: *¡Jesús!*, *¡Dios!*, *¡Por Dios!*, *¡Dios mío!*, *¡Santo Dios!*, and *¡Virgen!*.

5 Nouns

A noun is a word that identifies or stands for a specific person, place, thing, attribute, or action. A noun may also serve to sum up an idea, and a verbal form may serve as a noun on occasion. Nouns may be qualified by an adjective but never by an adverb. Proper nouns are those that designate a particular person, place, or thing (George, Jorge, Massachusetts, Costa Rica, the U.S.S. *Valiant*, etc.). Other possible categories of nouns are: common (any noun that does not qualify as a proper noun), collective (family, crowd, chorus, etc.), concrete (water, stone, mercury, and other objects perceived by the senses), and abstract (beauty, hope, despair, etc.).

PLURAL OF NOUNS

─────────────────── RULE ───────────────────

Spanish is similar to English in the manner in which nouns are made plural. However, unlike English, the forms of the Spanish articles show both gender and number (singular or plural). Nouns ending in a vowel usually add -*s* to form the plural; those ending in a consonant add -*es*.

───

Forming Plurals

Singular	Plural
el edificio (the building)	**los edificios** (the buildings)
la calle (the street)	**las calles** (the streets)
el avión (the airplane)	**los aviones** (the airplanes)
la ciudad (the city)	**las ciudades** (the cities)

PITFALL

Nouns ending in an accented -*í* or -*ú* usually add -*es* to form the plural. Those ending in -*á* or -*é* more often add only -*s*.

el rubí (ruby)		**los rubíes** (rubies)
el tabú (taboo)		**los tabúes** (taboos)
	but	
la mamá (mama)		**las mamás** (mamas)
el sofá (sofa)		**los sofás** (sofas)
el clisé (cliché)		**los clisés** (clichés)

PITFALL

Nouns ending in -*z* change the *z* to *c* before adding the plural -*es*.

la voz (voice)	**las voces** (voices)
el lápiz (pencil)	**los lápices** (pencils)
la vez (time)	**las veces** (times)

PITFALL

Nouns that have an unaccented final syllable ending in -*s* have the same form for both singular and plural.

la tesis (thesis)	**las tesis** (theses)
la crisis (crisis)	**las crisis** (crises)
el lunes (Monday)	**los lunes** (Mondays)
el paracaídas (parachute)	**los paracaídas** (parachutes)

PITFALL

The plural of many compound nouns (nouns composed of two elements) is formed in a regular manner. However, some show a plural change in both parts of the word, while others are invariable.

Regular:

el anteojo (telescope)	**los anteojos** (eyeglasses)
el ferrocarril (railroad)	**los ferrocarriles** (railroads)

el quitasol (parasol)	**los quitasoles** (parasols)
el sobretodo (overcoat)	**los sobretodos** (overcoats)

Change in both elements:

el gentilhombre (gentleman)	**los gentileshombres** (gentlemen)
el ricohombre (nobleman in old Castile)	**los ricoshombres** (noblemen)

Invariable (singular and plural the same):

el rascacielos (skyscraper)	**los rascacielos** (skyscrapers)
el parabrisas (windshield)	**los parabrisas** (windshields)
el rompecabezas (puzzle)	**los rompecabezas** (puzzles)

(Note that compound words like *rascacielos, parabrisas,* etc. are formed from the third person singular of the present tense of a verb + a plural noun. The gender is masculine even though the noun component may be feminine.)

PITFALL

Some words that have come into Spanish from other languages may have irregular plurals.

el club	**los clubes**
el complot (plot)	**los complots** (plots)
el lord	**los lores** (lords)
el déficit	**los déficit**

PITFALL

First names are regular when they are occasionally used in the plural, but last names are the same for singular and plural.

Los Juanes, Pedros y Antonios abundan mucho en México.
There are a lot of Johns, Peters, and Anthonys in Mexico.

Los Machado viven en la calle de Lope de Vega, 33, y la madre de la señora Machado vive muy cerca.
The Machados (Mr. and Mrs. Machado) live at No. 33 Lope de Vega Street, and Mrs. Machado's mother lives close by.

PITFALL

The plural form of some Spanish nouns is used where English employs a singular collective word. The singular forms of such words exist but cannot be used in a collective sense.

el dulce (piece of candy)	**los dulces** (candy)
el informe (report)	**los informes** (information)
el mueble (piece of furniture)	**los muebles** (furniture)
el negocio (piece of business)	**los negocios** (business, in a general sense)
la noticia (news item)	**las noticias** (news)
la vacación (holiday)	**las vacaciones** (vacation, holidays)

PITFALL

Los Estados Unidos (the United States), when considered as the name of one country, requires a singular verb.

Los Estados Unidos (or los EE.UU.) es un país muy grande y muy desarrollado.
The United States is a very large and very developed country.

PITFALL

Spanish singular collective nouns require a singular verb.

El pueblo mexicano es muy orgulloso.
The Mexican people are very proud. (Or: Mexicans are a very proud people.)

El coro del Teatro Liceo es el mejor de toda España.
The chorus of the Liceo Theater (Opera) is the best in all Spain.

But:

La mayoría de los estudiantes asistieron a la conferencia.
The majority of the students attended the lecture.

Accents

RULE

When nouns are made plural, the accented or stressed syllable does not change.

---

murciélago	**murciélagos**
lápiz	**lápices**
universidad	**universidades**
experiencia	**experiencias**

PITFALL

Only three Spanish nouns are exceptions and change their stress in the plural.

el carácter	**los caracteres**
el espécimen	**los especímenes**
el régimen	**los regímenes**

PITFALL

Sometimes the deletion or addition of a written accent mark is required in the plural form of a word (because a syllable has been added). Nouns ending in -*s* or -*n* with an accent on the last syllable usually drop the accent mark in the plural.

la lección	**las lecciones**

el ciprés	**los cipreses**
el entremés	**los entremeses**
la estación	**las estaciones**

PITFALL

Nouns of more than one syllable ending in -*n*, with no accent mark on the last syllable, add an accent mark in the plural to indicate that the stress has not been altered by the addition of -*es*.

el crimen	**los crímenes**
el joven	**los jóvenes**

GENDER

In English, nouns may be masculine, feminine, or neuter. Gender is, with few exceptions, equated with sex (male or female) and the majority of nouns that do not refer to persons are neuter gender since no sex identification is involved. *However, in Spanish nouns can be only masculine or feminine, and names for things are not neuter.* Although the words for male beings are generally masculine and those for female beings are feminine, it is best to disassociate the idea of grammatical gender from sexual identity in Spanish. The only Spanish "neuter" nouns are adjectives used with the article *lo* to express an abstraction (i.e. *lo bueno* the good part, what is good; *lo mejor*—the best part). (Also see section on Articles.)

Masculine Nouns

Nouns ending in -*o* are usually masculine gender. *(El primo, el lago, el tiempo, el verano, el zapato,* etc.). Exceptions are *la mano* and *la radio* which are feminine. *Mano* retains the feminine gender from the Latin *manus,* and radio is actually a shortened form of *radiodifusión* (*el radio* is also sometimes used and is a shortened form of *radio-receptor). La moto,* commonly used for "motorbike" or "motorcycle," is a shortened form of *la motocicleta;* and *la fotografía* is frequently shortened to *la foto.*

—————————— RULE ——————————

The names of **mountains**, **rivers**, **volcanoes**, etc., are usually masculine gender.

los Pirineos	**el Tajo**
los Andes	**el Támesis (Thames)**
el Danubio	**el Etna (volcano)**
el Amazonas	**el Misisipí**

—————————— RULE ——————————

The **days** of the week, the **months** of the year, and **languages** are masculine.

el viernes próximo	next Friday
el diciembre pasado	last December
el portugués	Portuguese

PITFALL

Although there are exceptions, many nouns ending in *-e, -í, -j, -l, -n* (not *ión), -r, -s,* and *-u* are masculine.

Endings	Nouns
-e	**el aceite, el alcalde, el escaparate, el fraile, el jefe, el padre, el chocolate, el cohete,** etc. (But: *la calle, la carne, la leche, la noche, la nieve,* and other feminine nouns ending in *-ie* and *-umbre.)*
-í	**el colibrí, el frenesí, el jabalí, el maravedí,** etc.
-j	**el reloj, el boj**

| -l | el árbol, el animal, el baúl, el cristal, el marfil, el plural, el rosal, etc. |

(But feminine exceptions such as: *la cárcel, la hiel, la miel, la piel, la señal, etc.*)

| -n | el ademán, el alacrán, el balcón, el carbón, el huracán, el plan, el tren, el violín, etc. |

(But feminine exceptions such *as: la sartén, la sazón, la sinrazón, la razón.*)

| -r | el altar, el amor, el dolor, el dólar, el humor, el olor, el sur, el valor, etc. |

(But feminine exceptions such as: *la flor, la labor,* and *la mujer.*)

| -s | el anís, el compás, el ciprés, el interés, el mes, el país, el vals, etc. |

(But feminine exceptions: *la crisis, la dosis, la hipótesis, la tos, la tesis, etc.*)

| -u | el espíritu, el tisú, el canesú, etc. |

(Exception: *la tribu.*)

PITFALL

A small number of nouns that end in *-ie* and *ión* are masculine gender.

el pie (foot)
el avión (airplane)
el aluvión (alluvion)
el bastión (bastion)
el centurión (centurion)

el gorrión (sparrow)
el limpión (wipe)
el sarampión (measles)
el turbión (squall)

PITFALL

The masculine plural of some nouns may be used to refer to members of both sexes.

mis tíos (my uncles *or* my uncles and aunts)
sus padres (his parents, his father and mother)

tus primos (your cousins—all male or both male and female)
tus primas (your cousins—all female)

Feminine Nouns

────────────────── RULE ──────────────────

Nouns ending in *-a*, *-dad*, *-tad*, *-tud*, *umbr*e, *-ie*, and *ión* are usually feminine.

──

la pluma	**la acción**
la ciudad	**la serie**
la libertad	**la costumbre**
la actitud	**la muchedumbre**

Note that the endings *-ción* and *-ión* correspond to the English *-TION* and *-ION*, *-dad* and *-tad* to the English *-TY*, and *-tud* to the English *-TUDE*.

PITFALL

Nouns ending in *-ma, -pa,* and *-ta* (which are of Greek origin) are always masculine gender unless they refer specifically to a woman.

el drama	**el tema**
el problema	**el mapa**
el programa	**el astronauta, la astronauta**
el teorema	**el diploma**

Adjectives modifying these words will, of course, show masculine agreement.

los mapas nuevos (not: **las mapas nuevas**) (the new maps)
el primer astronauta (the first male astronaut)
la primera astronauta (the first woman astronaut)
el drama serio (not: **el drama seria**) (the serious drama)

PITFALL

Although it ends in *-a,* the noun *día* (day) is masculine gender, and any adjective modifying this frequently used word must show masculine agreement if it ends in *-o.*

> *Buenos días* (not: **buenas días**) Good morning, good day
> *el tercer día del mes* (not: **la tercera día**) the third day of the month
> *Es otro día.* (not: **Es otra día.**) It's another day.

———————————— RULE ————————————

Nouns denoting **letters of the alphabet** are always feminine gender.

la A (the A)	**las Aes** (the A's)
la D (the D)	**las Des** (the D's)
la O (the O)	**las Oes** (the O's)

PITFALL

Some masculine nouns that end in *-o* and refer to persons have a feminine form ending in *-a* to identify persons of the female sex.

el abuelo (grandfather)	**la abuela** (grandmother)
el amigo (friend)	**la amiga** (friend)
el novio (boyfriend, fiancé)	**la novia** (girlfriend, fiancée)
el hijo (son)	**la hija** (daughter)
el tío (uncle)	**la tía** (aunt)
el primo (cousin)	**la prima** (cousin)
el cuñado (brother-in-law)	**la cuñada** (sister-in-law)
el suegro (father-in-law)	**la suegra** (mother-in-law)

PITFALL

Other nouns that are masculine gender have a comparable but distinct feminine form to identify persons of the female sex.

el actor (actor)	**la actriz** (actress)
el conde (count)	**la condesa** (countess)
el caballero (gentleman)	**la dama** (lady)
el hombre (man)	**la mujer** (woman)
el duque (duke)	**la duquesa** (duchess)
el príncipe (prince)	**la princesa** (princess)
el poeta (poet)	**la poetisa** (poetess)
el rey (king)	**la reina** (queen)

--- RULE ---

Nouns ending in *-ista* may be masculine or feminine depending on the sex of the person who is identified. Note that the *-ista* ending in Spanish corresponds to the English *-ist*.

---

el artista or **la artista**
el periodista or **la periodista**
el pianista or **la pianista**
el violinista or **la violinista**

PITFALL

Careful attention must be given to *-ista* words to avoid incorrect agreement of adjectives which are used as modifiers.

el artista famoso	or	**la artista famosa**
el pianista español	or	**la pianista española**
los artistas rusos	or	**las artistas rusas**

PITFALL

Certain other nouns have the same form for both masculine and feminine genders. Here again the article will indicate the sex of the person, but care must be given to correct agreement of adjectives.

el or **la cómplice** (accomplice)
el or **la estudiante** (student)
el or **la hereje** (heretic)
el or **la joven** (youth, young person)

el or **la mártir** (martyr)
el or **la modelo** (model)
el or **la testigo** (witness)
el or **la tigre** (tiger)
el or **la soprano** (soprano)

El cómplice fue   or   **La cómplice fue**
condenado.   **condenada.**
(The accomplice was sentenced.)

El se casó con una modelo muy guapa.
(He married a very pretty model.)

PITFALL

In recent years certain masculine words indicating professions are being given feminine forms in the spoken language because of the changing role of women in society.

el abogado	**la abogada**
el doctor	**la doctora**
el ingeniero	**la ingeniera**
el arquitecto	**la arquitecta**
el ministro	**la ministra**
el jefe	**la jefa**

PITFALL

Some nouns have masculine and feminine forms with different meanings. These words should be used with special attention to correct gender in order to avoid being misunderstood.

el arte—art, craft, appliance, artefact
los artes—the crafts
las artes—the fine arts
las malas artes—trickery

el capital—capital (money)
la capital—capital (city)

el canal—canal, TV channel
la canal—gutter

el cometa—comet
la cometa—kite

el cólera—cholera
la cólera—anger

el corte—cut, edge
la corte—court
las Cortes—Spanish parliament

el cura—priest
la cura—cure

el Génesis—book of the Old Testament
la génesis—origin or beginning

el frente—front (war)
la frente—forehead

el moral—mulberry tree
la moral—moral

el orden—order (arrangement), (law and) order
la orden—order (command)

el pendiente—earring
la pendiente—slope

el pez—fish
la pez—pitch, tar

el tema—theme, topic
la tema—fixed idea, mania

el coma—coma
la coma—comma

el policía—policeman
la policía—police (force)

el guía—guide (person)
la guía—guide (handbook)

PITFALL

Like English, Spanish sometimes has different words for the male and female of certain animals and birds.

el carnero (ram, sheep)	**la oveja** (eve, sheep)
el toro (bull)	**la vaca** (cow)
el gallo (rooster)	**la gallina** (hen)
but	
el pavo (turkey)	**la pava** (turkey hen)

With the names of animals, when the noun itself does not indicate the sex, *macho* (male) or *hembra* (female) may be used.

la ardilla macho	the male squirrel
el ruiseñor hembra	the female nightingale

INFINITIVES AS NOUNS

In English the infinitive and the present participle (gerund) of verbs can be used as nouns; in Spanish the infinitive is the *only* verbal form that can be used nominally, and it frequently occurs where the gerund (*-ing* form of the verb) would be required in English. The infinitive noun may be accompanied by the masculine article *el* or it may stand alone.

English:
          Inf.   Inf.
          To be or not to be is the question.

Spanish:
          Inf.   Inf.
          Ser o no ser es la cuestión.

English:
          Gerund   Gerund
          Seeing is believing.

Spanish:
          Inf.   Inf.
          Ver es creer.

	Gerund
English:	Too much dreaming is dangerous.

	Inf.
Spanish:	**El soñar demasiado es peligroso.**

	Gerund
English:	Upon getting off the train, he felt sick.

	Inf.
Spanish:	**Al bajar del tren, se sintió enfermo.**

6 Prepositions

A **preposition** is an invariable word used with a noun, pronoun, infinitive, or adverb to show a relationship to another word in a sentence or expression.

Preposition + noun	**para Juan** (for John)
Preposition + pronoun	**con él** (with him)
Preposition + infinitive	**antes de venir** (before coming)
Preposition + adverb	**desde ayer** (since yesterday)

─────────────── RULE ───────────────

The **prepositional phrase** normally serves as an adjective or adverb.

As an adjective:

el abrigo *de lana*
the wool coat

su método *de enseñar*
his teaching method

As an adverb:

Escríbame *antes del* 21 de abril.
Write me before the 21st of April.

***De ahora en adelante* voy a viajar.**
From today on I'm going to travel.

Simple and Compound Prepositions

Simple

a	to, at, for, by, on, from
ante	before, in the presence of
bajo	under, underneath
con	with
contra	against
de	of, from, about, with, by, in
desde	from, since, after
en	in, on, at, by
entre	between, among
hacia	toward, about, near
hasta	until, to, as far as, up to
para	for, to, towards
por	for, by, by means of, because of, for the sake of
según	according to
sin	without
sobre	about, on, upon, over, about
tras	after, behind

Compound

además de	in addition to, besides
alrededor de	around
antes de	before
cerca de	near
debajo de	underneath
después de	after
detrás de	behind, in back of
fuera de	outside of
lejos de	far from

PITFALL

Often the compound prepositions and the adverbs from which they are formed are confused. These prepositions would be incomplete and incorrect without *de*, and would instead be adverbs.

Adverb	Prepositions with *de*
además	**además de**
alrededor	**alrededor de**
antes	**antes de**
cerca	**cerca de**

INCORRECT SPANISH: **cerca el coche**

CORRECT SPANISH: *cerca del coche*
(near the car)

INCORRECT SPANISH: **debajo el árbol**

CORRECT SPANISH: *debajo del árbol*
(underneath the tree)

INCORRECT SPANISH: **dentro la caja**

CORRECT SPANISH: *dentro de la caja*
(inside the box)

PREPOSITIONS VERSUS CONJUNCTIONS

PITFALL

Some prepositions can also be confused with a similar conjunction. In English a preposition and the corresponding conjunction may be identical (and the specific function of the word is clear from its relation to other parts of the sentence or phrase). In Spanish there is always a distinct form for preposition and conjunction.

Prep.
↓

English: We'll go with you after the show.

Conj.
↓

We'll go with you after the show is over.

Prep.
↓

Spanish: **Iremos contigo después de la función.**

Conj.
↓

Iremos contigo después que termine la función.

Prep
↓

English: Before the 2nd of June the trip costs less.

Conj.
↓

Before the holidays begin, the trip costs less.

Prep.
↓

Spanish: **Antes del 2 de junio el viaje cuesta menos.**

Conj.
↓

Antes (de) que empiecen las vacaciones, el viaje cuesta menos.

CHOOSING THE CORRECT PREPOSITION

The choice of the appropriate Spanish preposition is sometimes difficult because the uses of a particular preposition frequently do not correspond to English usage. Certain verbs are always joined to a following infinitive by a particular preposition, but it must not be assumed that these verbs cannot be accompanied by other prepositions when they occur in different types of constructions. For example, the verb *ir* (to go) may occur with many prepositions, but the one most frequently used is *a*.

Voy *a* estudiar esta noche.
I'm going to study tonight.

Fuimos *al* cine anoche.
We went to the movies last night.

Van *de* Monterrey *a* Saltillo.
They're going from Monterrey to Saltillo.

Va *para* la estación.
He's going toward the station.

Fui *por* Miguel.
I went to get Michael.

Fueron *por* el parque.
They went through the park.

Irán *hasta* el río.
They'll go as far as the river.

Vamos *con* ellos.
Let's go with them.

The Preposition *a*

A is the most frequently used of the Spanish prepositions. Dictionary listings give its possible English meanings as: to, at, for, on, upon, in, into, by, and from.

USES OF *a*

1. The personal *a*: The use of the preposition *a* before noun direct objects referring to persons is probably the most difficult for the native speaker of English because there is no corresponding use in English:

    I don't know your friend Ramón.
    No conozco *a* tu amigo Ramón.

Daniel kissed his girlfriend.
Daniel besó *a* su novia.

That boy has made his parents suffer.
Ese chico ha hecho sufrir *a* sus padres.

2. The personal *a* is also required when the direct object is one of the indefinite pronouns which refer to persons *(alguien*—someone, somebody, *alguno(s)*—any(one), *nadie*—no one, nobody, *ninguno(s)* —none).

He's visiting someone in Guadalajara.
Está visitando *a* alguien en Guadalajara.

No conozco a nadie que trabaje tanto.
I don't know anyone who works so much.

3. The preposition *a* is often used to indicate separation in translating expressions such as "to take from," "to steal from," and "to buy from." The potential pitfall exists in the inclination of the English speaker to use *de* rather than *a*.

Le **quitaron *a* él sus documentos.**
They took his papers *from* him.

El ladrón *le* robó cien dólares *a* ese señor. (le = a ese señor)
The thief stole a hundred dollars *from* that gentleman.

¿Te **va a comprar la moto?**
(te = a ti)

Is he going to buy the motorcycle *from* you?
(or: ". . . to buy your motorcycle?")

4. *A* is required before noun indirect objects. Special attention must be paid to the verbs *gustar* (to be pleasing to, to like), *importar (to* matter to), and *faltar* (to be lacking to, to need), since they are

almost always used with an indirect object. (Note: *gustar* is not limited to third person subjects as is sometimes erroneously implied in basic language books; it is commonly used to express a liking for persons as well as things.)

Creo que *le* gusté *(a él)*.
I believe he liked me.

***A Juan le* gustan las películas argentinas.**
John likes Argentine films.
(But literally: "Argentine films are pleasing to John." Note that the sentence structure is quite unlike the most common English translation. The noun *películas* is the subject of *gustan* and both *le* and *a Juan* are the indirect object.)

Creo que *te* va a gustar la paella valenciana.
I think you're going to like Valencian *paella*.
(If *te* were replaced by a noun indirect object, *a* would always accompany the noun—*a María, a mi amigo, a los estudiantes*, etc.)
***A Carlos* no *le* importa la opinión de los otros.**
The opinion of others doesn't matter to Charles.

Maribel, *le* has gustado mucho *a mi amigo*.
Maribel, my friend liked you a lot.

5. After verbs of learning, beginning and teaching, *a* is required.

Estamos aprendiendo *a* hablar dos lenguas.
We are learning to speak two languages.

Se puso *a* leer (or: **Empezó *a* leer**.)
He began (started) to read.

Nuestro profesor nos enseñó *a* conjugar los verbos.
Our teacher taught us (how) to conjugate verbs.

6. The means or manner of doing something is expressed by *a*.

Lo hizo *a* mano.
He made it by hand.

Ella sabe escribir *a* máquina.
She knows how to type. (Literally: "to write by machine.")

7. Sometimes *a* is used in place of *por* in the sense of "for" to show feeling toward persons or things.

Aquellos héroes tenían mucho amor *a* su patria.
Those heroes had great love for their country (homeland).

8. *A* is used before expressions of price, speed, percent, and other measurements.

Estas naranjas se venden *a* seis pesos la docena.
These oranges sell (are sold) for six *pesos* a dozen.

El coche rojo corría *a* ciento veinte kilómetros la hora.
The red car was traveling at (a speed of) one hundred twenty kilometers an hour.

but compare:

Pisé el acelerador y me puse en ciento veinte.
I stepped on the accelerator and I hit a hundred twenty (kilometers an hour).

Common Phrases with *a*

a bordo	on board
a caballo	on horseback
al cabo, al fin	finally
a cada instante	at every turn
a casa	home (with verb of motion)
a causa de . . .	because of . . .
a la derecha (izquierda)	to the right (left)
a eso de . . .	about . . .
a espaldas	treacherously

a la larga	in the long run
a lo largo de ...	along ...
a lo lejos	in the distance
a menudo	frequently, often
a pesar de ...	in spite of ...
a pie	on foot
a pierna suelta	at one's ease, without a care
a poco de ...	a short while after...
a saltos	leaping, by leaps and bounds
a solas	alone
a tiempo	on time
a través de ...	through ...
a veces	sometimes

Verbs That Require *a* When Followed by an Infinitive or Other Dependent Element

acercarse a	to approach
acostumbrarse a	to become accustomed to
aficionarse a	to become fond of
alcanzar a	to succeed in (also used without *a* with noun object to reach, overtake, etc.)
aprender a	to learn how to
asistir a	to attend (school, a lecture, a play, etc.)
asomarse a	to look out of (window, door, etc.)
atreverse a	to dare to
comenzar a	to begin to
condenar a	to condemn to
dar a	to overlook (*dar* is also used alone with various meanings besides the basic "to give")
detenerse a	to pause to
dirigirse a	to address, speak to, go toward
disponerse a	to get ready to
echar(se) a	to start, to begin to
empezar a	to begin to
enseñar a	to teach to
invitar a	to invite to
jugar a	to play (sports, cards, etc.)
negarse a	to refuse to

obligar a	to oblige to
oler a	to smell like
parecerse a	to look like
ponerse a	to begin to
prepararse a	to prepare to
resolverse a	to make up one's mind to
saber a	to taste of
sonar a	to sound like
subir a	to get into (vehicle)
venir a	to attain, to end up by
volver a	to . . . again

PITFALL

After the verb *tener* (to have) the personal *a* is normally not used.

> **Tengo tres hermanos.**
> (I have three brothers.)

> **Tienen amigos que viven en México.**
> (They have friends who live in Mexico.)

PITFALL

A frequent problem in Spanish expression is the choice of *a* or *en* to mean "at." *A* may mean "at" occasionally, but more frequently *en* is required.

> **Elisa se quedó *en* casa ayer.**
> Elisa stayed at home yesterday.
> (Never *a* except in sense of "to" with verbs of motion.)

> **Elisa fue *a* casa ayer.**
> Elisa went home yesterday.

> **Estudiamos *en* la Universidad de Missouri.**
> We study *at* the University of Missouri.
> (Never *a* except in sense of "to" with verbs of motion.)

> **Vamos *a* la universidad todos los días.**
> We go *to* the university every day.

On the other hand, *a* rather than *en* may mean "on" in certain expressions.

> **Siempre llega *a* tiempo.**
> He always arrives *on* time.

> **Pensamos subir la montaña *a* pie.**
> We intend to go up the mountain *on* foot

The Preposition *ante*

Ante means "in front of" or "before" in the sense of "in the presence of."

> **El se levantó ante el juez.**
> He stood up before the judge.

> **Ante su abuela ella no se atrevía a hablar.**
> She didn't dare speak in the presence of her grandmother.

The Preposition *bajo*

Bajo has both the literal and figurative meaning of "under," but it can never mean "underneath" in the physical sense.

> **México cambió mucho bajo el gobierno de López Mateos.**
> Mexico changed a great deal under the government of López Mateos.

> **Dormían bajo los árboles.**
> They were sleeping under the trees.

PITFALL

Bajo is sometimes confused with *debajo de*. The latter means "underneath" in a literal, physical sense.

> **Jardiel Poncela es el autor de la comedia *Eloisa está debajo de un almendro*.**
>
> Jardiel Poncela is the author of the play *Eloise is Underneath an Almond Tree*.
> (*i.e.* literally buried under the tree)

To avoid unintentional humor, care must be taken in the translation of an English sentence such as: "I would like to study under Professor Gómez." *Debajo de* would, of course, be totally inappropriate. A prudent Spanish rendering would be: *"Quisiera estudiar con el profesor Gómez."*

The Preposition *con*

Con is the equivalent of the English preposition "with." It is also frequently used with a noun to form an adverbial phrase. (See section on Adverbs.)

> **El ciego tiene que andar con cuidado.**
> The blind man must walk carefully.

(Here *con cuidado* is a substitute for the adverb *cuidadosamente*.)

Verbs Followed by *Con*

acabar con	to put an end to, to finish off
casarse con	to marry
conformarse con	to resign oneself, to put up with
contar con	to count on
contentarse con	to be satisfied with
cumplir con	to fulfill
encontrarse con	to meet (by chance), run into
entenderse con	to come to an understanding with
meterse con	to pick a quarrel with
soñar con	to dream of (about)
tropezar con	to run into (collide)

PITFALL

Verbs such as *casar (se)* and *soñar* frequently cause difficulties for the English-speaking student because of an inclination to translate literally from English to Spanish. Compare the following examples with the English equivalents.

Mi amigo Carlos sueña con casarse con una estrella del cine.
My friend Charles dreams of marrying a movie star.

Elena se casó con un astronauta.
Elena married an astronaut.

Los padres de Elena la casaron con un astronauta.
Elena's parents married her off to an astronaut.

Elena y el astronauta se casaron el 3 de junio.
Elena and the astronaut got married the 3rd of June.

PITFALL

Note that __*con + mí*__ (with me) becomes *conmigo;* __*con + ti*__ (with you) becomes *contigo;* and __*con + sí*__ (with him, her, you, himself, etc.) becomes *consigo.*

Ven conmigo. (not: **con mí**)
Come with me.

Siento no poder ir contigo. (not: **con ti**)
I'm sorry not to be able to go with you.

El hombre lleva el pasado consigo. (not: **con sí**)
Man carries the past with him.

The Preposition *contra*

Contra means "against" and denotes opposition to someone or something, either in a literal or figurative sense.

La universidad está contra la carretera.
The university faces (is opposite) the highway.

Los moros luchaban contra los cristianos.
The Moors fought against the Christians.

El Presidente habló contra el miedo.
The President spoke against fear.

The Preposition *de*

De may mean "of," "from," "about, or "by." It often expresses possession, origin, and the material of which something is made. After nouns, the preposition is usually *de*.

Possession: **Esta es la casa del presidente.**
This is the president's house.

Quiero presentar a la amiga de Raúl.
I want to introduce Raul's friend.

Origin: **Los Rubio son de Cuba.**
The Rubios are from Cuba.

Material: **Esta blusa es de seda**
This blouse is (of) silk.

Mi padre me regaló un reloj de oro.
My father gave me a gold watch.

PITFALL

De sometimes means "with" or "in" when it links a word to a more or less inseparable characteristic or personal effect.

Vimos rezar a *la vieja del vestido negro*.
We saw the old woman in the black dress praying.

***El señor del acordeón* siempre toca en esta esquina.**
The man with the accordion always plays on this corner.

However, *con* is used when the descriptive phrase indicates a characteristic or personal effect that is not considered inseparable from the person.

El hombre con el revólver **va a robarnos el dinero.**
The man with the gun (in his hand) is going to take our money from us.

PITFALL

De + an infinitive phrase sometimes takes the place of an "if" clause expressing an idea contrary to fact.

De haberle visto antes, no habría salido.
If I had seen him before, I would not have left.

PITFALL

De must follow a superlative in Spanish to translate the English "in."

Son las joyas más codiciadas *del* mundo.
They're the most desired jewels in the world.

Es el río más largo *de* Europa.
It's the longest river in Europe.

PITFALL

In English an infinitive (to + verb) frequently follows a noun as a modifier. In Spanish, *de* is required between the noun and infinitive in such constructions unless the infinitive answers the question: "For what purpose?" Then *para* is required rather than *de* to link noun and infinitive modifier.

It's *time to get up.*
Es *la hora de levantarse.*

Norelco makes an excellent electric razor.
Norelco fabrica una *excelente máquina de afeitar eléctrica.*
(an excellent machine for shaving)

Buscamos *un lugar para esquiar.*
We're looking for *a place to ski.* (for the purpose of skiing)

Common Expressions with *de*

de acuerdo	in agreement
de buena gana	willingly
de día	by day, in the daytime
de día en día	from day to day
de esta manera	in this way
de hoy en adelante	from today on
de mal humor	in a bad humor
de memoria (with **aprender**)	(to learn) by heart
de moda	in style
de nada	you're welcome, it's nothing
de ningún modo	in no way, by no means
de noche	by night, at night
de nuevo	again
de otra manera	in another way
de pie	standing
de prisa	in a hurry
de pronto	suddenly
de repente	suddenly
de rodillas	kneeling
de todos modos	anyway, at any rate
de veras	really
de vez en cuando	from time to time

Verbs Commonly Followed by *de*

abusar de	to abuse, overindulge in
acabar de + inf.	to have just + past participle
acordarse de	to remember, recall
alegrarse de	to be happy about
apartarse de	to move (keep) away from
aprovecharse de	to take advantage of
burlarse de	to make fun of, to mock
cambiar de (ropa, avión, tema, etc.)	to change (clothes, planes, subject, etc.)

cansarse de	to get tired of
carecer de	to lack
cesar de	to stop
compadecerse de	to pity, feel sorry for
constar de	to consist of
cuidar de	to care for, take care of
deber de	must, ought to
dejar de	to stop, leave off
depender de	to depend on
despedirse de	to take leave of, to say goodbye to
disfrutar de	to enjoy
enamorarse de	to fall in love with
enterarse de	to find out about
fiarse de	to trust
gozar de	to enjoy
haber de	to be supposed to, be to
ocuparse de	to attend to (a task)
olvidarse de	to forget
preocuparse de	to worry about
quejarse de	to complain about
reírse de	to laugh at
servir de	to serve as, to be used as
tratar de	to try to
tratarse de	to deal with, be a question of

Many of the verbs listed above pose problems for the English-speaking student because they do not represent literal translations of the English equivalent. Some are reflexive verbs that do not have reflexive counterparts in English. For example, the Spanish *"Me enamoré de ella,"* does not literally mean "I fell in love with her" but rather "I enamoured myself of her." A literal translation of the correct English sentence would result in an unintelligible sentence in Spanish. Note, however, that in the Spanish verb *enamorar* we find the same basic components (*en + amor*) that we have in the English expression. A similar comparative analysis of the English and Spanish in each case can prevent incorrect expression or faulty translations.

PITFALL

Acabar de **+ an infinitive** is the Spanish equivalent of the English **"to have just"** + **a past participle**. A comparison of the English and Spanish constructions will aid in a clearer understanding of the differences.

Present Perfect Tense
(with elements separated by "just")

English: I *have* just *eaten* dinner.

Present Indicative   Infinitive of verb
of *acabar*   conveying main idea

Spanish: **Acabo de cenar.**

Past Perfect Tense
(with elements separated by "just")

English: I *had* just *eaten* dinner.

Imperfect   Infinitive of
Indicative of   verb conveying
acabar + *de* +   main idea

Spanish: **Acababa de cenar.**

PITFALL

Another troublesome Spanish idiom with *de* is *haber de* **+ infinitive** which describes the type of mild obligation expressed in English by **"to be to"** + **infinitive** or by **"to be supposed to"** + **infinitive**.

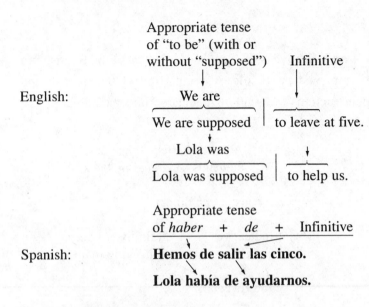

English:

Appropriate tense of "to be" (with or without "supposed") — Infinitive

We are

We are supposed | to leave at five.

Lola was

Lola was supposed | to help us.

Spanish:

Appropriate tense of *haber* + *de* + Infinitive

Hemos de salir las cinco.

Lola había de ayudarnos.

The Preposition *desde*

Desde translates the English "from" in phrases relating to time or place.

> **Desde el 19 hasta el 23 de mayo asistiremos a conferencias sobre la arquitectura azteca.**
> *From* the 19th until the 23rd of May we'll attend lectures on Aztec architecture.

> **Van *desde* México a Guadalajara en tren.**
> They're going *from* Mexico City to Guadalajara by train.

The Preposition *en*

En is commonly used in expressions of **time**, **place**, and **means**, as well as serving to link certain verbs to dependent elements.

> **Vivíamos *en* Santiago.**
> We used to live *in* Santiago.

> **Ahora vivo *en* el número 22 de la calle Bolívar.**
> Now I live *at* number 22, Bolívar Street

Este conflicto empezó *en* el siglo pasado.
This conflict began *in* the last century.

El tren acaba de entrar *en* la estación.
The train has just entered (into) the station.

PITFALL

En is the *only* preposition that may be followed by a present participle *(gerundio)*, and in such cases it has the sense of "after" (+ the English gerund).

***En escribiendo* la carta, la dejó en el escritorio.**
After writing the letter, she left it on the desk.

PITFALL

The expressions *en mi vida* and *en absoluto* have negative meanings and do not require the "never," "not," or "nothing" that are necessary in the English translation.

***En mi vida* he visto tal cosa!**
Never in my life have I seen such a thing!

¿Lo vio usted ayer? *¡En absoluto!*
Did you see him yesterday? *Absolutely not!*

PITFALL

Both *en* and *a* are sometimes used to translate the English "at" and care must be given to the correct choice.

Hace tres años que estudio *en* esta universidad.
I've been studying *at* this university for three years.

Me quedo *en* casa los lunes.
I stay at home on Mondays.

But:

El arquitecto está sentado *a* su escritorio.
The architect is seated *at* his desk.

La función de noche comienza _a_ las once.
The evening show begins _at_ eleven.

Common Expressions with _en_

en alto	up, high (up)
en balde	in vain
en broma	in fun
en casa	at home
en caso de	in case of
en cuanto	as soon as
en cuanto a	as for
en esto	at this point
en lo alto de	up, on top of
en lugar de	in place of
en marcha	under way
en medio de	in the middle of
en ninguna parte	nowhere
en punto	sharp (with time expressions)
en seguida	immediately
en suma	in short
en torno de	around, about
en vez de	instead of
en vilo	in the air, undecided

Verbs Commonly Followed by _en_

complacerse en	to be pleased to, to delight in
confiar en	to trust (in), rely on, be confident about
consentir en	to consent to
consistir en	to consist of
convenir en	to agree to
empeñarse en	to insist on
entrar en	to enter
esforzarse en	to try hard to, to strive

fijarse en	to notice
insistir en	to insist on
meterse en	to get into, plunge into
pensar en	to think about (consider)
quedar en	to agree on
tardar en	to delay in, to be late in

The Preposition *entre*

Entre translates the English "between" and "among."

> ***Entre* las 2,30 y las 3,00, alguien rompió la ventana.**
> *Between* 2:30 and 3:00 a.m., someone broke the window.

> **Pasó diez años *entre los* árabes.**
> He spent ten years *among* the Arabs.

PITFALL

Subject pronouns rather than object pronouns are used after *entre* (also after *incluso* and *según*). These include *yo* and *tú* in place of *mí* and *ti*.

> ***Entre tú y yo,* no creo lo que está diciendo.** (not **Entre ti y mí**. . .)
> *Between you and me*, I don't believe what he is saying.

> ***Entre mis amigos y yo,* no hay secretos** (not **Entre mis amigos y mí**)
> *Between my friends and me,* there are no secrets.

The Preposition *hacia*

Hacia means "toward" or "about" in expressions of place or time.

> **Caminamos *hacia* el parque.**
> We walked toward the park

> ***Hacia las* 2 de la mañana empezó a llover.**
> About (toward) two a.m. it began to rain.

The Preposition *hasta*

Hasta means "till," "until" and "as late as" in expressions of time; "as far as," "up to," and "down to" in expressions of place; "as much as" or "as many as" in expressions of quantity.

No llegará *hasta* la medianoche.
He won't arrive until midnight

Fueron *hasta* la orilla del Pacífico.
They went as far as the shore of the Pacific

***Hasta* 400.000 toneladas de carbón han sido exportadas cada año.**
As many as 400,000 tons of coal have been exported each year.

Common Expressions with *hasta*

hasta ahora	up until now
hasta después (entonces)	until later, see you later
hasta la vista	goodbye, see you later
hasta luego	
hasta mañana	until tomorrow, see you tomorrow
hasta más no poder	to the utmost
hasta no más	

The Prepositions *para* and *por*

Although both *para* and *por* translate the English "for," they cannot be used interchangeably. Their uses are quite distinct and frequently subtle.

PARA

——————————— RULE ———————————

Generally, *para* is used to express purpose ("in order to") or to point toward a certain place or a time or action in the future (in relation to the main verb of the sentence).

Purpose:	**Hay que creer *para* tener éxito.** One must believe (in order) to have success.
	Está estudiando *para* salir bien en el examen. He's studying in order to do well on the test.
Destination:	**Saldrán *para* San Antonio el martes.** They'll leave for San Antonio on Tuesday.
	Este regalo es *para* ella. This gift is for her.
Time:	**Tenemos una cita *para* el sábado.** We have a date for Saturday.
	Volverá *para* el 3 de abril. He'll return by the 3rd of April.

―――――――――――――――― RULE ――――――――――――――――

Para is also used to express an implied comparison.

―――――――――――――――――――――――――――――――――――――

***Para* un estudiante del segundo año, habla muy bien.**
For a second year student, he speaks very well.

(The statement suggests that the student speaks well in comparison to other students of the second year.)

―――――――――――――――― RULE ――――――――――――――――

Para is used to denote use for which a thing is intended.

―――――――――――――――――――――――――――――――――――――

Este camino es *para* uso limitado.
This road is for limited use.

Estos platos son *para* el postre.
These plates are for the dessert.

PITFALL

Note the difference between *una taza de café* and *una taza para café*. The former means "a cup of coffee," while the latter means "a coffee cup," or "a cup used for coffee."

una taza de té	a cup of tea
una taza para té	a teacup
un vaso de agua	a glass of water
un vaso para agua	a water glass

Common Expressions Using *para*

estar para . . .	to be about to . . .
no estar para bromas	not to be in the mood for joking
no ser para tanto	not to be so important
para con	towards (a person)
para siempre	forever

POR

———————————————— RULE ————————————————

Among the several uses of *por* are: to express the agent of a verb in the passive voice (by); to indicate a lapse of time (for); to show obligation or concern for a person (for, for the sake of, on behalf of); to indicate mode of transportation (by), velocity or frequency (per), and manner (with). This preposition also occurs in many idiomatic expressions.

Agent: **Este ensayo fue escrito *por* Marañón.**
This essay was written *by* Marañón.

Esta novela ha sido leída *por* millones de españoles.
This novel has been read *by* millions of Spaniards.

Time lapse or duration:	**Los astronautas estuvieron en la luna *por* ocho horas.** The astronauts were on the moon *for* eight hours.
	Mi primo estudió en la Argentina *por* dos años. My cousin studied in Argentina *for* two years.
Obligation, concern and duty:	**Lo hizo *por mí*.** He did it *for me*. (for my sake or on my behalf)
	Siempre lucharán *por* la libertad. They'll always fight *for* freedom.
	Acompañé a mi hermanita *por* mi madre. I accompanied my little sister *for* my mother. (because my mother asked me to)
Mode of transportation or transmission:	**Prefieren viajar *por* avión.** They prefer to travel by plane.
	Esta noche hablaremos *por* teléfono móvil. Tonight we'll talk by cellular telephone.
Velocity, frequency:	**El límite de velocidad es cien kilómetros *por* hora.** The speed limit is a hundred kilometers *per* hour.
	Asistimos a esta clase dos veces *por* semana. *We attend this class two times per week.*
Manner:	**Victoria los vio por sus propios ojos.** Victoria saw them *with* her own eyes.

--------------------- RULE ---------------------

Por is also used to show the **aim**, **purpose**, or **motive** of an action.

Fue *por* María.
He went to get Mary. (to pick her up)

Han ido *por* gasolina.
They've gone for gas.

Abandonó la ciudad *por* miedo.
He left the city out of fear.

Le otorgaron el premio *por* su primera obra.
They awarded him the prize for his first work.

PITFALL

Por is sometimes used with an infinitive to indicate that an action has yet to be completed—or that the outcome of the action is uncertain.

Quedan dos capítulos *por* escribir.
Two chapters remain to be written.

El contrato está *por* firmarse.
The contract is yet to be signed.

———————————— RULE ————————————

Por is also used in expressions that indicate an opinion held by someone about a person or a thing.

Me tiene *por* persona de pocas palabras.
He considers me a person of few words.

Le dejaron *por* muerto.
They left him for dead. (They believed him to be dead when they left.)

———————————— RULE ————————————

Por is also used in the sense of "through," "along," and "in exchange for."

Cantaban mientras se paseaban *por* el parque.
They were singing as they strolled through the park.

Los amantes caminan *por* la orilla de este lago azul.
Lovers walk along the shore of this blue lake.

Les pagamos ocho mil dólares *por* el SEAT.
We paid them eight thousand dollars for the SEAT
(Spanish-manufactured car).

PITFALL

Por means "because of," and the English-speaking student sometimes erroneously creates an artificial form *porque de* by translating directly from English. Such a form does not exist in Spanish.

English:	He had to give up his studies because of the war.
INCORRECT SPANISH:	**Tuvo que dejar sus estudios porque de la guerra.**
CORRECT SPANISH:	***Tuvo que dejar sus estudios por la guerra.*** (or *"a causa de la guerra"*)

Common Expressions with *por*

por aquí	this way
Por Avión	Air Mail
por consiguiente	consequently
por desgracia	unfortunately
por Dios	for heaven's sake
por eso	therefore
por escrito	in writing
por favor	please
por fin	finally, at last
por la mañana (tarde, noche)	in (during) the morning (afternoon, night)
por lo menos	at least
por lo tanto	therefore
por lo visto	apparently
por mi parte	as far as I'm concerned

por poco	almost, nearly
por regla general	as a general rule
por mi cuenta	to my way of thinking
por supuesto	of course
por todas partes	everywhere
al por mayor	wholesale
al por menor	retail

Verbs Commonly Followed by *por*

acabar por	to end up by
dar por	to consider
darse por	to pretend to
estar por	to be in favor of
interesarse por	to take an interest in
pasar por	to be considered
tener por	to consider (have an opinion on)
tomar por	to take someone for

CONTRASTIVE USES OF *PARA* AND *POR*

1. **Estudié *para* el examen.**
   I studied for the exam (*i.e.,* for the purpose of taking the exam).

   Estudié *por* el examen.
   I studied because of the *exam* (*i.e.,* because the exam was hanging over my head).

2. **Ella le dio 100 pesetas *para* el pan.**
   She gave him 100 pesetas for the bread (so that he could go buy it).

   Ella le dio 100 pesetas *por* el pan.
   She gave him 100 pesetas for the bread. (She paid him the pesetas in exchange for the bread.)

3. **Eduardo compró el anillo *para* su novia.**
   Edward bought the ring for his girlfriend. (He bought it to present to her.)

Eduardo compró el anillo *por* su novia.
Edward bought the ring for his girlfriend. (He bought it as a favor for her. The ring may be intended for another person. It is not a gift from Edward to his girlfriend.)

4. **Andan *para* el Prado.**
They are walking in the direction of the Prado.

   Andan *por* el Prado.
They are walking through (or around) the Prado.

5. **Vamos a Puerto Vallarta *para* un mes de vacaciones.**
We're going to Puerto Vallarta for a month's vacation. (Here only the idea of a vacation is stressed and not the period of time.)

   Vamos a Puerto Vallarta *por* un mes.
We're going to Puerto Vallarta for a month. (The period of a month is the point of emphasis.)

6. **Es muy activo *para* su edad.**
He's very active for his age. (He is an eighty-year-old person who gets around very well, considering his age.)

   Es muy activo *por* su edad.
He's very active because of his age. (He's a five-year-old child and naturally lively.)

The Preposition *sin*

Sin is the equivalent of the English "without."

> **El tipo ese salió *sin* pagar la cuenta.**
> That character left without paying the bill

PITFALL

Sin is sometimes used with an infinitive to describe something that has not yet been done. In English, such a description is frequently expressed by an adjective beginning with the prefix "un."

> **La casa está *sin pintar*.**
> The house is unpainted.

Tienen muchas cuentas *sin pagar.*
They have a lot of unpaid bills.

PITFALL

Double negatives are correct in Spanish, and because *sin* has a negative force, it is often followed by another negative.

Salió *sin* ver a *nadie*.
He left without seeing anyone.

Llegó *sin* sombrero *ni* impermeable.
He arrrived without (a) hat or (a) raincoat.

The Preposition *so*

PITFALL

So means "under" but is archaic today in Spanish except when combined with *capa, pena,* or *pretexto.*

so capa de	under the guise of
so pena de	on pain of
so pretexto de	under the pretext of

Entraron so pretexto de buscar al reo.
They entered under the pretext of seeking the criminal.

The Preposition *sobre*

Sobre means "on," "over," "upon," "about," and "on the subject of."

Escribió una tesis doctoral *sobre* el teatro de Griselda Gambaro.
He wrote a doctoral thesis on (the subject of) the theater of Griselda Gambaro.

El bolígrafo que perdiste está *sobre* (or en) la mesa.
The ballpoint that you lost is on (top of) the table.

(Note that *encima de* and *por encima de* also mean "over" or "above.")

Se podían ver los fuegos artificiales *encima del* castillo antiguo.
The fireworks could be seen over the ancient castle.

The Preposition *tras*

PITFALL

Tras means "after" or "behind" but only to indicate the order in which one person or thing follows another person or thing.

Día *tras* día trabajaba en las minas.
Day after day he worked in the mines.

Ella siguió andando *tras* él.
She continued walking behind him.

VERBS WITHOUT PREPOSITIONS

Some Spanish verbs are not followed by a preposition at all, even though their English equivalents always require a preposition before a dependent or related element.

agradecer	to thank for
	Le agradecimos su bondad.
	(*bondad* is the direct object of the verb; *le* is the indirect object.)
	We thanked him for his kindness.
	(*him* is the direct object; *kindness* is the object of the preposition *for.*)
aprovechar	to take advantage of
	Espero que aproveches la oportunidad.
	(*oportunidad* is the direct object of the verb.)
	I hope you'll take advantage of the opportunity.
	(*opportunity* is the object of the preposition *of.*)

buscar   to look for (*or* to seek)

Tengo que buscar el dinero que perdí.
(*dinero* is the object of *buscar*.)
I have to look for the money I lost.
(*money* is the object of the preposition *for.*)

(Note that when *buscar* is translated as "seek" the Spanish and English constructions are grammatically the same: *La he buscado en todas partes.*—I've sought her everywhere.)

conseguir   to succeed in

¿Conseguiste obtener el disco?
(verb is followed by a direct infinitive)
Did you succeed in obtaining the record?
(the gerund *obtaining* is the object of the preposition *in*)

(Note, however, that the linking preposition is not required if the translation of *conseguir* is "manage" rather than "succeed.")

escuchar   to listen to

Pablo estaba escuchando esa canción popular de Miguel Bosé.
(*canción* is the direct object of the verb)
Paul was listening to that popular song (sung) by Miguel Bosé.
(*song* is the object of the preposition *to*)

esperar   to wait for

Te esperé media hora.
(*te* is the direct object of the verb)
I waited for you half an hour.
(*you* is object of the preposition *for*)

lograr   to succeed in

Logró realizar sus sueños.
(verb takes a direct infinitive)
He succeeded in realizing his dreams.

(the gerund *realizing* is the object of the preposition *in*)

mirar to look at (*or* to watch)

Están mirando la luna.
(*luna* is the direct object of the verb)
They are looking at the moon.
(*Moon* is object of the preposition *at*)

(However, when *mirar* is translated as "watch" or "behold," the Spanish and English constructions are grammatically the same: *Todas las noches miramos la televisión*—Every night we watch television.)

pagar to pay for

Pagó el billete.
(*billete* is the direct object of the verb)
He paid for the ticket.
(*ticket* is object of *for*)

Note, however, the change in construction that occurs when the amount paid is introduced into the sentence:

Pagó mil pesetas por el billete.
(*pesetas* is now the object of the verb and *billete* becomes object of the preposition *por*)
He paid a thousand pesetas for the ticket.
(The English and Spanish constructions are now the same.)

pedir to ask for (or to request)

Voy a pedirle una Coca Cola.
(*Coca Cola* is the direct object and *le* is the indirect object.)
I'm going to ask him for a Coke.
(*him* is the object of the verb [infinitive] and *Coke* is the object of the preposition *for*.)

(Note that the Spanish and English constructions are similar when *pedir* is translated as "request.")

7 Pronouns

Pronouns are usually described as "words that stand for nouns." In short, a pronoun has an antecedent—a word or idea, a person or thing, to which it refers—and in most cases the antecedent is known to the speaker. If the pronoun is interrogative (who?, which?, what?) the speaker is requesting the identity of the antecedent. If the pronoun is negative (nobody, nothing, etc.), the antecedent is, of courses non-existent.

TYPES OF PRONOUNS
PERSONAL PRONOUNS
Spanish has a different set of personal pronouns for subjects of verbs, direct objects of verbs, indirect objects, and reflexive objects. An additional set serves as the objects of prepositions.

Subject Pronouns

yo (I)
tú (you)
él (he, it)
ella (she, it)
usted (you)
nosotros (as) (we)
vosotros (as) (you)
ellos (as) (they)
ustedes (you)

Direct Object Pronouns

me (me)
te (you)
le (him), **lo** (him, it)
la (her, it)
le, lo, la (you)
nos (us)
os (you)
los, las (them)
los, las (you)

Indirect Object Pronouns

me (to me)
te (to you)
le (to him, her, it, you)

nos (to us)
os (to you)
les (to them, you)

Reflexive Object Pronouns

me (myself)
te (yourself)
se (himself, herself, itself, yourself)
nos (ourselves)
os (yourselves)
se (themselves, yourselves)

Object of Prep. Pronouns

(para) mí (for me)
(para) ti (for you)
(para) él (for him, it)
(para) ella (for her, it)
(para) usted (for you)
(para) nosotros (as) (for us)
(para) vosotros (as) (for you)
(para) ellos (as) (for them)
(para) ustedes (for you)

PITFALL

Since the subject and object pronouns (direct, indirect, and reflexive) are used in direct conjunction with a verb (before or after), they are sometimes called "conjunctive pronouns." The pronouns used as objects of prepositions are called "disjunctive" because they are always separated from the verb.

Subject Pronouns

PITFALL

Except for *usted* and *ustedes* (formal "you"), Spanish subject personal pronouns are used much less frequently than their English equivalents. Unlike English verbs, Spanish verbs convey clearly the person and number of the subject in their endings. Excessive use of the subject pronouns can seem formal to the point of rudeness. However, on occasion the pronoun is necessary for emphasis.

(Yo) Tengo cien dólares y (yo) voy a gastarlos.
I have a hundred dollars and I'm going to spend them.

(*Yo* is unnecessary and undesirable with both verbs since both *tengo* and *voy* are unmistakably first person singular.)

Ustedes pueden pasar ahora.
You can come in now.

(Since *pueden* may also be used with *ellos* and *ellas*, *ustedes* is needed for comprehension. It is also included in the sentence for courtesy. However, *usted* and *ustedes* should not be needlessly repeated once the fact that they govern the verb is clear to the person addressed.)

Dicen que se casó con Pepe. No lo creo yo.
They say that she married Joe. *I* don't believe it

(Here *yo* is included in the second sentence for emphasis. Note that it acquires greater force by following the verb.)

PITFALL

Spanish has four forms for the single English subject pronoun "you." These cannot be used interchangeably, and they pose special problems for English-speaking students. *Tú* and *vosotros (as)* are the singular and plural second person forms normally used when speaking to friends, relatives, and children. *Usted* and *ustedes* are third person forms (derived from *vuestra merced,* "your grace," and *vuestras mercedes,* "your graces") which are used for more formal exchange. *Usted* and *ustedes* are sometimes used with close associates to show respect but *tú* is the rule in informal contacts. A shift from *tú* to *usted* when speaking to a friend would also indicate anger or displeasure.

On the other hand, the use of *tú* when addressing a superior or an older person might suggest contempt. *Ustedes* is normally used in place of *vosotros* in the Spanish-speaking countries of the Western hemisphere for familiar address. In Spain, however, *vosotros* is a normal and necessary form when speaking to a group of intimates or to children. For example, a conversation among a group of Spanish university students who are acquainted would require the use of second person plural verbs (with *vosotros*). It would seem ludicrous to address small children as *"ustedes."* Examples of the everyday use of *vosotros* can be found in modern plays, novels, television, films, and comic strips.

Carlos, ¿cuándo piensas volver?
Charles, when do you intend to come back?
(The second person singular form is required because the speaker is on a first name basis with the person addressed.)

Amigos, ¿queréis ir a la playa conmigo?
Friends, do you want to go to the beach with me?
(The second person plural form is required because the speaker is addressing a group of his friends. In the Spanish of the Western Hemisphere, *queréis* would become *quieren (ustedes)*.)

Abuelita, pareces muy triste.
Grandmother, dear, you seem very sad.
(The speaker is addressing his grandmother in an affectionate manner.)

Señor, usted tendrá que esperar hasta más tarde.
Sir, you will have to wait until later.
(The speaker is addressing an unidentified person in a formal manner.)

Padre, necesito el dinero y usted debe prestármelo.
Father, I need the money, and you must lend it to me.
(Although a son is speaking to his father, the nature of the conversation indicates formality, and the situation may well be tense.)

Señores y señoras, tengo el gusto de presentarles al nuevo presidente.
Ladies and gentlemen, I have the pleasure of presenting to you the new president.
(Clearly a formal address)

Direct and Indirect Object Pronouns

Spanish direct and indirect object personal pronouns normally are placed directly before all verb forms except present participles, infinitives, and affirmative commands. In the case of participles, the pronoun(s) may be attached to the participle or they may precede the auxiliary verb (*estar*, *ir*, *etc.*). With affirmative commands the pronoun object is always attached at the end. When a verb has both direct and indirect objects that are pronouns, the indirect always precedes the direct. Whenever two third person pronouns beginning with the letter "l" occur together, the first (the indirect object) changes to *se (le > se* and *les > se)*. This is done for greater ease of pronunciation.

Direct Object:	**¿Dónde está Elisa? No *la* veo.** Where is Elisa? I don't see *her*.
(with infinitive)	**Pablo, quiero ayudar*te*.** Paul, I want to help *you*.
(with present participle)	**Había tantas estrellas, y estábamos mirándo*las* toda la noche.** (or: . . . y *las* estábamos mirando toda la noche. There were so many stars, and we were looking at *them* all night.
(with affirmative command)	**Juan, ayúda*me*, por favor.** John, help *me*, please.
(with negative command)	**Juan, no *me* ayudes, por favor.** John, don't help *me*, please.

Direct and Indirect Objects:	**¿Dónde está mi libro? ¿No *me lo* devolviste anoche?** Where is my book? Didn't you return *it to me* last night?
(with infinitive)	**Pablo, quiero mostrár*telo* ahora.** Paul, I want to show *it to you* now.
(with present participle)	**Está leyéndo*noslo* para que aprendamos el diálogo de memoria.** or: ***Nos lo* está leyendo. . .)** He is reading *it to us* so that we will learn the dialogue by heart.
(with affirmative command)	**Señor, léa*noslo* otra vez.** Sir, read *it to us* again.
(with negative command)	**Señor, no *nos lo* lea ahora.** Sir, don't read *it to us* now.

Two 3rd person objects—
indirect direct:

Juan tiene el suéter azul.
***Se lo* devolví (a él) ayer.**
John has the blue sweater. I returned *it to him* yesterday.

(In the example above, *se* has been substituted for *le* (to him) because it is followed by a second pronoun beginning with "l." For clarification *a él* may be included in the sentence but it is not essential.)

PITFALL

In Spanish, the **indirect object** pronoun sometimes has the sense of "from" (rather than "to" or "for") when used with the verbs *comprar, quitar,* or *robar*.

Spanish:	**El policía *le* quitó la pistola.**
English:	The policeman took the pistol *from him*.

Spanish:	***Nos* compró el terreno en Morelia.**
English:	He bought the land in Morelia *from us*.

Reflexive Pronouns

Reflexive objects always stand for the same person or thing— noun or pronoun—that is subject of the verb. The verb may also have a noun or pronoun direct object, but in one way or another the action of the verb is directed by the subject back toward the subject itself. Many Spanish verbs that are normally used with reflexive objects do not require a reflexive construction in English translation. (Also see section on Verbs.)

> **Me levanté y me vestí.**
> I got up and I got dressed.
> (But literally: "I raised myself (up) and I dressed myself.")

> **Jorge *se* quitó la camisa y *se* lavó las manos.**
> George took off his shirt and washed his hands.
> (But more literally: "George took from himself the shirt and washed to himself the hands.")

PITFALL

At times the reflexive pronoun is used to intensify or otherwise change the meaning of a Spanish verb. Such constructions cannot be translated *literally* into English.

> (non-reflexive)
> Compare: **Bebimos el vino y fuimos a otro restaurante.**
> We drank the wine and went to another restaurant.

> (reflexive)
> **Nos bebimos el vino y nos fuimos a otro restaurante.**

We drank up the wine and went off to another restaurant.

(non-reflexive)
Vi a Tony después que volvió.
I saw Tony after he returned.

(reflexive)
Vi a Tony después que se volvió.
I saw Tony after he turned around.

PITFALL

Se, *nos*, and *os* are frequently used in a reciprocal sense to translate the English "each other."

Jorge y Ramón se vieron en la feria.
George and Raymond saw each other at the fair.

Nos miramos y nos enamoramos.
We looked at each other and fell in love.

Hijos míos, debéis escribiros pronto.
My children, you should write each other soon.

(Phrases such as *uno a otro, unos a otros, el uno al otro, el uno a la otra, etc.,* may be used to clarify reciprocal constructions, but in most cases they are unnecessary and can cause a sentence to seem awkward.)

Ahora Carlota y Ana se miran. Or,
Ahora Carlota y Ana se miran una a otra.
Now Charlotte and Anna are looking at each other.

Objects of Prepositions (Disjunctive Pronouns)

——————— RULE ———————
Except for *mí* (me) and *ti* (you) objects of prepositions are identical to the subject pronouns. The forms *conmigo* and *contigo* are used when *mí* or *ti* are used as objects of the preposition *con*.

Estábamos charlando *con ella.*
We were chatting *with her.*

Ella no va a casarse *contigo.*
She's not going to marry *you.* ("with" does not occur in the English sentence)

Este paquete es *para usted;* **ése es** *para nosotros.*
This package is *for you;* that one is *for us.*

PITFALL

Frequently the disjunctive pronouns are used with the preposition *a* to clarify or to emphasize an indirect object pronoun.

A ella **le gusta nadar.**
She likes to swim. (Literally: "To swim is pleasing to her:")

Ahora me toca *a mí.*
Now it's *my* turn.

POSSESSIVE PRONOUNS

—————————————— RULE ——————————————

Possessive pronouns are formed in Spanish by adding the definite article to the long form of the possessive adjective. (The article is usually omitted when the pronoun follows any form of the verb *ser.*) Possessive pronouns always agree in number and gender with the thing (or person) possessed (and *not* the possessor).

POSSESSIVE PRONOUNS

el mío, la mía, los míos, las mías—mine
el tuyo, la tuya, los tuyos, las tuyas—yours (singular)
el suyo, la suya, los suyos, las suyas—his, hers, yours (sing.)

el nuestro, la nuestra, los nuestros, las nuestras—ours
el vuestro, la vuestra, los vuestros, las vuestras—yours (plural)
el suya, la suya, los suyos, las suyas—theirs, yours (plural)

Rita, este bañador es *mío*; *el tuyo* está en el coche, pero Juan ha dejado *el suyo* en casa.
Rita, this bathing suit is *mine; yours* is in the car, but John has left *his* at home.
(The article is omitted with *mío* because the pronoun follows a form of the verb *ser; el tuyo is* masculine because it refers to *bañador*—even though the possessor, *Rita,* is feminine.)

¿Me prestarás tu cámara? José tiene *la mía*.
Will you lend me your camera? Joseph has *mine.*
(Although the speaker may be a male, *la mía* is feminine because it refers to *cámara)*

Sus hijos están de vacaciones; *los nuestros* se han quedado en casa.
Their children (sons and daughters) are on vacation; *ours* have stayed at home.
(los nuestros is masculine plural because it refers to *hijos.)*

PITFALL

El suyo (and its feminine and plural forms) may stand for any third person (his, hers, theirs, yours). Since it is not always clear *which* third person is involved, *suyo* may be replaced by *de él, de ella, de ellos, de ellas, de usted,* or *de ustedes* to avoid confusion or ambiguity.

Este bañador es mío; *el de ella* está en el coche.
This bathing suit is mine; *hers* is in the car.
(Although *el suyo* would be correct too, *el de ella* makes clear beyond any question the identity of the possessor.)

DEMONSTRATIVE PRONOUNS

———————————— RULE ————————————

Demonstrative pronouns point out a specific person or thing. The Spanish forms are identical to those of the demonstrative adjectives except that each form bears a written accent on the stressed syllable to distinguish it from the adjective.

Estos libros son baratos; *ésos* **cuestan más.**
These books are cheap; *those* cost more.

Quisiera escuchar otro disco; *éste* **no me gusta.**
I'd like to listen to another disc; I don't like *this one*.

DEMONSTRATIVE PRONOUNS

éste, ésta—this, this one
ése, ésa—that, that one
aquél, aquélla—that, that one
éstos, éstas—these
ésos, ésas—those
aquéllos, aquéllas—those

PITFALL

There are also three neuter demonstratives (*esto, eso, aquello*) which are used only to sum up an idea. Since they have no adjective counterparts, they do not require the distinguishing accent mark. These forms can never be used to refer to a person or thing.

Se fue sin decírmelo, y *esto* **me preocupa mucho.**
He left without telling me, and *this* bothers me a great deal.
(Here *esto* refers to the whole idea of his leaving without saying anything about it.)

Recuerde *esto:* **Si desea recibir una gran atención personal vuele por Iberia.**

Remember *this:* If you wish to receive real personal attention, fly Iberia.
(Here *esto* refers to the total idea expressed in the statement that follows.)

***Eso* de ayer nos interesó mucho.**
That business of yesterday (what happened yesterday) interested us a lot.

PITFALL

When referring back to two people or things mentioned in a previous sentence, English frequently uses the words "former" and "latter." In Spanish the demonstratives *éste (ésta)* and *aquél (aquélla)* are employed for the same purpose. *Aquél* = former because it means "that one"—the one first mentioned and consequently the more distant grammatically speaking; *éste* = latter because it means "this one"—the one mentioned last in the sentence and, consequently, the closer in the order of presentation. Note how *éste (ésta)* always comes first in Spanish.

English: *Louisa* and *Raymond* got married in Marbella.

   The *former* is Spanish and the *latter* is Portuguese.

Spanish: **Luisa y Ramón se casaron en Marbella.**

   ***Este* es portugués y *aquélla* es española.**

English: I've just read two novels by Galdós:
   Doña Perfecta and *La desheredada.*

   The *former* was written in 1876 and the *latter* in 1881.

Spanish: **Acabo de leer dos novelas de Galdós:**
   Doña Perfecta* y *La desheredada.

   ***Esta* fue escrita en 1881 y *aquélla* en 1876.**

RELATIVE PRONOUNS

──────────────── RULE ────────────────

The basic function of relative pronouns is to join one clause with another. The most frequently used Spanish relative is *que*, which may mean "who," "that," "which," or "whom." It may refer to either persons or things, and it may be either singular or plural.

> *La flor de mi secreto* **es la película** *que* **inauguró las proyecciones.**
> *The Flower of My Secret* is the film *that* began the showings.

> **He visto las películas** *que* **le gustaron tanto a usted.**
> I have seen the films *that* you liked so much.

PITFALL

Que is commonly used with the prepositions *a, con, de,* and *en* to refer to a thing or a place. It is *not* normally used with the longer prepositions.

> **El avión** *en que* **viajábamos aterrizó en Lima.**
> The plane *in which* we were travelling landed in Lima.

PITFALL

Note that the preposition *always* comes immediately before *que* regardless of the word order that may be acceptable in an English translation.

English: The beach *that* I was speaking *of* is fantastic.
Spanish: **La playa** *de que* **hablaba es fantástica.**

(Remember that *que* is one of the most versatile words in Spanish, and that it is not used solely as a relative. In comparisons it means "than"; as a conjunction "that" or "for"; when introducing indirect questions, "let.")

Other Spanish Relative Pronouns

PITFALL **Quien, Quienes**

Quien and its plural, *quienes,* are used only in reference to persons. They may replace *que* in nonrestrictive clauses (i.e., nonessential and set off by commas), and are required after prepositions when referring to persons. They are also used in an introductory position to translate the English expressions "he who," "the one(s) who," "those who," etc.

> **El rey Alfonso XIII, *quien* abdicó en 1930, murió fuera de España.**
> King Alfonso XIII, *who* abdicated in 1930, died outside of Spain.

> **Los señores *de quienes* hablaba le esperan en el aeropuerto.**
> The gentlemen *of whom* I was speaking are waiting for you at the airport

> ***Quien* tiene dinero debe tener tiempo para gastarlo.**
> *He who (the man who)* has money should have time for spending it.

PITFALL **El que, El cual**

El que, *El cual*, and their feminine and plural forms, are frequently used in place of *que* when specific gender identification is desirable, and as objects of prepositions. They may also be substituted for *quien(es)* in nonessential clauses or in the introductory position to translate "he who," "the one(s) who," "those who," etc.

> **Este pintor, *el que* estudió en Barcelona, vive ahora en México.**
> *(el cual, quien* or even *que* would also be correct in the nonrestrictive clause.)
> This painter, *who* studied in Barcelona, lives in Mexico now.

Los que **tienen dinero deben saber gastarlo.**
Those who have money should know how to spend it.

Hay tres ventanas grandes *por las cuales* **se ve el campo silencioso.**
There are three large windows *through which* one sees the silent countryside.

PITFALL **Lo que, Lo cual**

Lo que and *lo cual* are neuter relative pronouns that may be used only to refer to ideas or complete statements—and *never* to specific persons or things.

Lo que **usted me propone es muy interesante.**
What you're proposing to me is very interesting.

Ella se puso a recitar el poema, *lo cual* **no me impresionó mucho.**
She began to recite the poem, *which* didn't impress me very much.
(Here *lo cual* refers to the action of reciting the poem.)

PITFALL **Cuyo**

Cuyo is the Spanish relative that means "whose." It must agree in number and gender with the noun that follows.

Es un director *cuyas* **películas son famosas por toda Europa.**
He's a director *whose* films are famous throughout Europe.

El mundo de Sofía, cuyo **tema es la filosofía, fue la novela más vendida de 1995 en España.**
Sophie's World, whose theme is philosophy, was the best-selling novel of 1995 in Spain.

INTERROGATIVE PRONOUNS

Interrogative pronouns introduce questions. The Spanish interrogatives are:

INTERROGATIVE PRONOUNS

¿qué. . . ? what. . . ?
¿cuál. . . ? ¿cuáles. . . ? which (one). . . ? which (ones). . . ?
¿quién(es). . . ? who. . . ?
¿de quién(es). . . ? whose. . . ?
¿cuánto (a, os, as) . . . ? how much (many) . . . ?

¿*Qué* es la vida? *What* is life?
(An explanation or definition is sought.)

¿*Cuál* de los vestidos te gusta más?
Which of the dresses do you like best?
(Here the identification of one of several possibilities is requested.)

¿*Cuáles* son las obras más conocidas de Rubén Darío?
Which (ones) are the best known works of Rubén Darío?

¿*Quién* es el protagonista de *Luces de bohemia?*
Who is the protagonist of *Bohemian Lights?*

¿*Quiénes* eran los Reyes Católicos?
Who were the "Reyes Católicos"?

¿*De quién* es el Fiat azul?
Whose blue Fiat is that?
(or "To whom does the blue Fiat belong?")

¿*Cuánto* cuesta el viaje a Puerto Rico?
How much does the trip to Puerto Rico cost?

Tengo quinientas pesetas. ¿*Cuántas* necesitas?
I have five hundred pesetas. *How many* do you need?

PITFALL

Cuyo (whose) is used only as a relative and may never be used as a substitute for *¿de quién?*

INCORRECT SPANISH: **¿Cuyo reloj de pulsera es éste?**
CORRECT SPANISH: ***¿De quién es este reloj de pulsera?***
Whose wristwatch is this?

PITFALL

The interrogatives *¿por qué?* and *¿para qué?*, composed of a preposition + *qué,* both translate the English "why." The former asks the reason or motive for an action; the latter seeks the identification of the goal or outcome of an action.

> ***¿Por qué* no quisiste ayudarme?**
> *Why* did you refuse to help me?

> ***¿Por qué* se ha detenido el tren?**
> *Why* has the train stopped?

> ***¿Para qué* estudian ustedes tanto?**
> *Why* do you study so much? (What is your goal?)

> ***¿Para qué* fue inventada esta máquina curiosa?**
> *Why* (for what?) was this odd machine invented?

PITFALL

When a question is expressed in an indirect manner or merely implied, the interrogative pronoun may occur within a sentence rather than as the introductory word. It retains its accent mark.

> **Me preguntaron *qué* deseaba.**
> They asked me *what I* wanted.

> **No *sé cuál* de éstas prefiero: la falda azul o la roja?**
> I don't know *which* of these I prefer: the blue skirt or the red one?

INDEFINITE AND NEGATIVE PRONOUNS

Common Spanish Indefinite Pronouns

algo	something
alguien	somebody, someone
alguno(s)	some (one)

Hay *algo* que no comprendo.
There is *something* (that) I don't understand.

***Alguien* le ha dicho la verdad.**
Someone has told her the truth.

Había leído de los claveles de Granada, y al llegar compré *algunos*.
I had read about the carnations of Granada, and when I arrived I bought *some*.

Aprendieron de memoria *algunos* de los poemas.
They memorized *some* of the poems.

Common Spanish Negative Pronouns

nada	nothing
nadie	nobody, no one
ninguno (a, os, as)	no one, none

***Nada* le gusta más que esquiar.**
Nothing pleases him more than skiing.

Es un placer que a *nadie* hace daño.
It's a pleasure that harms *no one*.

***Ninguna* de estas joyas vale más de mil pesetas.**
None (not one) of these jewels is worth more than a thousand pesetas.

PITFALL

Whenever a negative pronoun follows the verb, *no* must precede the verb, producing a double negative construction. However, since the double negative is incorrect in English usage, the indefinite pronoun will become positive in translation.

> **Ya *no* recuerdo *nada* del accidente.**
> I no longer remember *anything* about the accident.

> ***No* conocieron a *nadie* en la fiesta.**
> They didn't meet *anyone* at the party.

PITFALL

After a comparative, indefinites require the negative form in Spanish.

> **Juan me quiere más que *nadie*.**
> John loves me more than *anyone*.

> **Más que *nada* me gusta viajar.**
> I like to travel more than *anything*.

PITFALL

Both the indefinite *alguien* and its negative *nadie* require the "personal *a*" when used as direct objects.

> **Esta mañana no he visto a *nadie*.**
> This morning I've seen no one. (Or, this morning I haven't seen anyone.)

8 Verbs

All verbs, both regular and irregular, are subject to changes of *person* (3 singular and 3 plural forms), *tense* (14 in Spanish), and *mood* (indicative or subjunctive). Some verbs may also undergo a change of *voice*—that is, a change from active to passive.

The basic form of every verb is its infinitive. For each verb there are also two participles: present and past. Although a number of common verbs are irregular in formation, the majority of Spanish verbs fall into three basic groups or conjugations: (1) those with an infinitive ending in *-ar (tomar* - to take); (2) those whose infinitive ends in *-er (vender* - to sell); and (3) those ending in *-ir (vivir* - to live). Changes in the verb are effected by dropping the infinitive ending and adding appropriate endings to the stem by adding an ending to the entire infinitive, or by using the past and present participles with an auxiliary or helping verb which indicates person, tense, and mood.

PERSON

A Spanish verb may be governed by the person speaking (1st person), the person or persons spoken to (2nd person familiar "you" or 3rd person formal "you"), or the person(s) or thing(s) spoken about (3rd person). Verbs are third person when the subject is a noun. Although in Spanish, as in English, there are pronoun forms to indicate person. These pronouns are used less frequently than in English, since *unlike English* the person is usually apparent in the verb ending. Excessive and unnecessary use of personal subject pronouns is considered bad usage in Spanish and can give an undesired emphasis to a statement.

(Also see section on Personal Pronouns.)

yo (I)   **nosotros** (as) (we)
tú (you)   **vosotros** (as) (you)
él (he, it)   **ellos** (as) (they)
ella (she, it)   **ustedes** (you-formal)
usted (you-formal)

Anoche *(yo)* estudié hasta las once.
Last night *I* studied until eleven o'clock.
(In English the *I* is absolutely essential for comprehension; in Spanish the person and tense are both indicated in the 1st person preterite ending *-é*. Yo is unnecessary and undesirable in the sentence (except for emphasis).

***Ella* cantaba en Buenos Aires.**
She used to sing in Buenos Aires.
(In the 3rd person it may be necessary to use the subject pronouns for clarity, but if the person spoken about is clear from the context, then the pronoun may be omitted.)

PITFALL

In English the single pronoun "you" takes care of all 2nd person situations, singular or plural. However, Spanish has four ways of speaking directly to people—two that are truly second person, and two that are used with third person forms of the verb.

1. *Tú* ("you" singular familiar) is used almost universally when speaking to one's immediate family, to children, to animals, and above all to close friends. It is not a form limited to younger people but is heard among close acquaintances of all ages. (It is also true that *usted* (formal "you") is also employed among certain people who could be considered friends and, on occasion, even between husband and wife.) There is no absolute guide for the appropriate use of the so-called "intimate" form *tú,* but it is always safe to use it with people one's own age who use it first in conver-

sation. Spanish has a special verb *(tutearse)* which means "to speak to one (another) in the familiar form."

> **Enrique y Carmen** *se tutean* **ahora.**
> Henry and Carmen address each other familiarly now.
> (However, a freer and more appropriate translation would be: "Henry and Carmen are on close terms now.")

2. *Vosotros (as)* is the plural form of *tú*. It is composed of the older Spanish pronoun *vos + otros (as)* and is not unlike the "you all" heard in some parts of the United States. Although this form is rarely heard in the Spanish-speaking areas of the Western Hemisphere, where *ustedes* is substituted for all plural second person address, it is an essential form in Spain. It must be mastered if one is to speak correct Spanish in Europe or read and comprehend the literature of Spain. (Beware of textbooks that omit this form!)

> (Note: For an explanation of the use of *vos* as a singular pronoun in the Spanish of the Río de la Plata region of South America, see section on Dialects and Variations of Spanish.)

3. *Usted.* This peculiar looking word is really a contraction of two longer words: *vuestra merced* (your grace). This explains why it governs a 3rd person verb. It began as a very formal 3rd person, indirect type of personal address and has come to be the normal form of "you" employed in business and with anyone who is not a close associate. (Originally, the formal form of singular address was *vos,* minus the *otros.* It was similar to the French *vous.*)

4. *Ustedes*, the plural form of *usted,* is a contraction of *vuestras mercedes* (your graces) and is used with a 3rd person plural verb to speak to more than one person on a formal basis and also (in Latin America only) to speak to two or more intimates.

PITFALL

Do not mix *tú* and *usted,* or *vosotros* and *ustedes* (or their related object, possessive pronoun and adjective forms) when addressing the same person or persons.

INCORRECT SPANISH: **Pablo, tengo tu cartera y usted tiene la mía.**

CORRECT SPANISH: *Pablo tengo tu cartera y (tú) tienes la mía.*
(Paul, I have your wallet and you have mine.)

INCORRECT SPANISH: **Niños, debéis acostarse ahora.**

CORRECT SPANISH: *Niños, debéis acostaros ahora.*
(Children, you should go to bed now.)

VERB TENSES *(TIEMPOS DEL VERBO)*

The Spanish word for tense is *tiempo* (time), and a change of tense represents a change of time in the action described by a verb. There are fourteen verb tenses in Spanish; seven are simple—*i.e.* the verb form consists of a single word; and seven are compound—composed of the appropriate form of the verb *haber* (to have) plus the past participle of the verb. Although these comprise a verb system very closely akin to that of English, attempts to equate each Spanish tense with an English counterpart can lead to pitfalls of usage. In many instances a literal translation of an English verb form into Spanish results in an incorrect or even an unintelligible statement; and by the same token, literal translations of Spanish forms can produce absurd English.

THE INDICATIVE TENSES

Indicative Tenses

Present	**hablo**	I speak, I do speak, I am speaking
Preterite	**hablé**	I spoke, I did speak
Imperfect	**hablaba**	I used to speak, I was speaking

Future	**hablaré**	I shall speak
Conditional	**hablaría**	I would speak
Present Perfect	**he hablado**	I have spoken
Past Perfect	**había hablado**	I had spoken
Preterite Perfect	**hube hablado**	I had spoken
Future Perfect	**habré hablado**	I shall have spoken
Conditional Perfect	**habría hablado**	I would have spoken

Present *(Presente del Indicativo)*

——————————————— RULE ———————————————

Formation: The endings *-o, -as, -a, -amos, -áis, -an* are added to the stem of regular *-ar,* verbs; *-o, -es, -e, -emos, -éis, -en* are added to the stem of regular *-er,* verbs; and *-o, -es, -e, -imos, -ís, -en* are added to the stem of regular *-ir* verbs. (Special peculiarities of irregular verbs can be noted in the table of irregular verbs.)

Use: To describe an action that is taking place at the time the word is spoken.

———————————————————————————————————————

¿En qué *piensas? Pienso* en las vacaciones.
What are you thinking about? I'm thinking about (my) vacation.

PITFALL

Like English, Spanish has progressive forms of the tenses but these are used less frequently than in English. When the progressive form occurs, the action described is immediate and in progress in terms of the context of the statement. (Also see section on Present Participles.)

¿Qué hace usted aquí? *Estoy esperando* a mis amigos.
What are you doing here? I am waiting for my friends.

——————————————— RULE ———————————————

Use: The present tense is also used to describe an action that will take place in the near future.

———————————————————————————————————————

Nos *vemos* a las dos de la tarde.
We'll see each other at two in the afternoon.

Mañana *salgo* para España.
Tomorrow I leave for Spain.

RULE

Use: The present is used in time expressions to describe an action that began in the past and continues into the present. (Also see detailed explanation under Time Expressions.)

Hace cuatro horas que María *escucha* esos discos de música sinfónica.
Mary has been listening to those recordings of symphonic music for more than four hours.

Lo *espero* desde hace veinte minutos.
I've been waiting for him for twenty minutes.

Imperfect and Preterite Tenses (Imperfecto y Pretérito del Indicativo)

The imperfect and preterite are both simple past tenses, but they cannot be used interchangeably. The **imperfect** describes an action begun in the past (which may have ended already or which may well be continuing into the present) without regard for the specific beginning or termination of the action. Several English translations are possible, depending on the context (English simple past, past progressive, "used to," and "would"). The **preterite** tense describes a single action or several actions that occurred at a fixed time in the past. When the preterite is used, there is no possible question about the complete termination of the action in the past—even though the action may have occurred over a period of time. It is helpful to consider the two tenses separately and then together.

RULE

Formation: The imperfect is formed by adding the endings *-aba, -abas, -aba, -ábamos, -abais, -aban* to the stem of first conjugation *-ar* verbs;

the endings *-ía, -ías, -ía, -íamos, -íais, -ían* are added to the stems of both second conjugation *-er* verbs and third conjugation *-ir* verbs.

Imperfect: Time

Past   Present   Future

Juan trabajaba los sábados.
John worked (used to work) on Saturdays.
(repeated action but no reference to beginning or termination)

Carlos estudiaba más que yo.
Charles used to study more than I.
(action continued over an indefinite period)

Estaba nevando y hacía un frío espantoso.
It was snowing and it was frightfully cold.
(action in the past unfixed by time limits)

─────────────── RULE ───────────────

Formation: To form the **preterite** tense, the endings *-é, -aste, -ó, -amos, -asteis, -aron* are added to the stem of *-ar* verbs; *-í, -iste, -ió, -imos, -isteis, -ieron* are added to the stems of both *-er* and *-ir* verbs.

Preterite: Time

                                                            Past

Ayer tuve un examen en química. ⟶
Yesterday I had an exam in Chemistry.

Se encontró con Lola anoche. ⟶
Last night he ran into Lola.

Escribí una carta a mi madre. ⟶
I wrote a letter to my mother.   Present

(Each action is fixed in the past and
clearly terminated)   Future

Imperfect and Preterite together:

The following sentences, which contain verbs in both the imperfect and preterite tenses, illustrate the basic differences in use:

> **Juan** *se puso* **el impermeable porque** *llovía.*
> John put on his raincoat because it was raining.

> *Estaba durmiendo* **cuando** *sonó* **el teléfono.**
> I was sleeping when the telephone rang.

> **Casona vivía en Buenos Aires cuando** *se estrenó* **La dama del alba.**
> Casona was living in Buenos Aires when *La dama del alba* was performed for the first time.

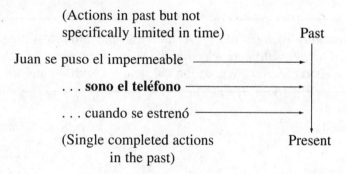

Past   Present   Future

. . . porque llovía
Estaba durmiendo . . .
Casona vivía en Buenos Aires

(Actions in past but not
specifically limited in time)   Past

Juan se puso el impermeable ⟶

. . . sono el teléfono ⟶

. . . cuando se estrenó ⟶

(Single completed actions   Present
in the past)

Other Uses

PITFALL

Any emotional state or mental activity in the past normally is described in the imperfect. (However, the preterite may be used when the speaker desires to convey the idea that the state or activity is decidedly over.)

Carlos creía que ella lo quería.
Charles believed that she loved him.

Sabía que no tenía razón.
I knew that he wasn't right.

Lo dudaba pero no estaba seguro.
I doubted it but I wasn't sure.

But:

Está muy triste ahora porque lo quiso tanto.
She's very sad now because she loved him so much.
(It's all over.)

RULE

The imperfect is used in narration to describe characteristics and conditions and to set the scene in the past.

Era una noche de invierno. Hacía frío y brillaban las estrellas. Los soldados esperaban el amanecer y nadie dormía.
It was a winter night. It was cold and the stars were shining. The soldiers were waiting for daybreak and no one was sleeping.

RULE

The imperfect is used in time expressions to describe an action that began in the past and that continued over a period in the past. (Also see detailed explanation under Time Expressions.)

Hacía cuatro horas que María escuchaba esos discos de musica sinfónica.
Mary had been listening to those recordings of symphonic music for four hours.

Lo esperaba desde hacía veinte minutos.
I had been waiting for him for twenty minutes.

RULE

The imperfect is also used in simple time statements in the past.

Eran las cinco cuando empezó la corrida.
It was five o'clock when the bullfight began.

Era temprano cuando nos levantamos.
It was early when we got up.

PITFALL

Certain common Spanish verbs have their normal meanings in the imperfect tense but special meanings when used in the preterite.

Quería . . .	I wanted, I loved.
Quise. . .	I tried (*also* I wanted, I loved)
No quería . . .	I didn't want, I didn't love
No quise . . .	I refused
Conocía . . .	I knew
Conocí . . .	I met (by introduction)
No podía . . .	I couldn't
No pude . . .	I didn't succeed in
Sabía . . .	I knew
Supe . . .	I found out
Tenía . . .	I had
Tuve . . .	I got, received

Le pedimos que nos explicara sus palabras, pero *no quiso*.
We asked him to explain his words to us, but he refused.

Mi bisabuelo conocía a Pancho Villa. Lo conoció en Chihuahua.
My great-grandfather knew Pancho Villa. He met him in Chihuahua.

Trató de detener el coche pero no pudo.
He tried to stop the car but he failed (couldn't).

Ayer tuve una carta de Costa Rica.
Yesterday I received a letter from Costa Rica.

Future *(Futuro del Indicativo)*

──────────────────────── RULE ────────────────────────

Formation: The endings *-é, -ás, -á, -emos, -éis, -án* are added to the *entire* infinitive. It is actually the addition of the present tense of the verb *haber*, with the silent *h* dropped and a slight modification in the 2nd person plural. (*Tomar-he* has become *tomaré*. This accounts for the accents on the endings consisting of one syllable.)

Use: The future tense in Spanish has the same meaning as its English counterpart. It describes an action that has yet to take place. Remember, however, that in Spanish the present tense is frequently used to describe an action that is to occur in the near future.

──

Usted me *llamará* muchas veces todavía y yo *acudiré* siempre.
You will still call me many times, and I shall respond (to your call) always.

***Sé que volverá* a contarme la misma historia.**
I know that he will tell me the same story again.

PITFALL

The future has a special use in Spanish that is frequently misread by the English-speaking student. This use, commonly called the "future of probability," has numerous possible English translations. A literal translation is always incorrect and *must be avoided*.

¿Qué *pensará* este señor?
(Although pensará normally means "will think," here conjecture is involved. Possible English translations would be: "I

wonder what this man is thinking." "What can this man be thinking?" "What do you suppose this man is thinking?")

¿Qué hora *será? Serán* las seis y pico.
What time can it be? It's probably a little after six.
(Again a literal translation is impossible, and the structure of the English rendering is quite different from that of the Spanish.)

PITFALL

When dealing with supposition or conjecture, special attention must be paid to translation from English to Spanish to avoid awkward expression.

English:	Someone is crying out. Who do you suppose it is?
INCORRECT SPANISH:	**Alguien grita. ¿Quién supones que es?**
CORRECT SPANISH:	*Alguien grita. ¿Quién será?*

PITFALL

The future is *not* used to make a request as in English. Rather the present of *querer* + an infinitive is required.

English:	Will you sit down, Inspector?
INCORRECT SPANISH:	**¿Se sentará, señor comisario?**
CORRECT SPANISH:	*¿Quiere sentarse, señor comisario?*

English:	Will you shut up!
INCORRECT SPANISH:	**¿Te callarás?**
CORRECT SPANISH:	*¿Quieres callarte?*

Conditional *(Condicional)*

—————————————— RULE ——————————————

Formation: The conditional tense is formed by adding the endings *-ía, -ías, ía, -íamos, -íais, -ían* to the entire infinitive. These endings are the same as those that are added to the stems of *-er* and *-ir* verbs to form the imperfect.

Use: The conditional is used to translate the English "would" + an infinitive (English conditional tense) except when "would" indicates habitual past action.

Estaba seguro de que no *llegarían* para las cinco.
I was sure that they wouldn't arrive by five o'clock.

¿Te dijeron que *costaría* tanto?
Did they tell you that it would cost so much?

Si no estuviera lloviendo, *iríamos* a la playa.
If it were not raining, we would go to the beach.

PITFALL

Unlike English, the Spanish conditional does not describe a habitual past action. In such expressions the imperfect is required.

English:	I remember them well. They would get up at six o'clock, eat breakfast, and study until time for the first class.
INCORRECT SPANISH:	**Los recuerdo bien. Se levantarían a las seis, se desayunarían, y estudiarían hasta la hora de la primera clase.**
CORRECT SPANISH:	*Los recuerdo bien. Se levantaban a las seis, se desayunaban, y estudiaban hasta la hora de la primera clase.*

PITFALL

As in English, the conditional is sometimes used for politeness to avoid the bluntness of the present tense.

> **Me *gustaría* visitarlos en diciembre.**
> I'd like to visit you in December.

> **¿Le *gustaría* probar este plato?**
> Would you like to try this dish?

> **¿*Podría* usted decirme el número del señor Ruiz?**
> Could you give me the number of Señor Ruiz?

PITFALL

Like the future, the conditional is used to express conjecture or probability (past probability as opposed to the present probability of the future tense).

> **Yo no la conocía, pero *sería* muy guapa.**
> I didn't know her, but she was probably very good looking.
> (or: "I imagine she was very good looking.")

> **¿Cómo *obtendría* Juan el dinero? Se lo *prestaría* su padre.**
> How do you suppose (I wonder how) John got the money?
> His father probably lent it to him. (or: "I suppose his father lent it to him.")

PITFALL

The Spanish conditional does not translate the English "should" when obligation is intended. In such cases the Spanish auxiliary *deber* (should, ought to, must) is required.

English:	You should consider the advantages of our service before choosing.
Spanish:	**Usted debería (or: debe, debiera) considerar las ventajas de nuestro servicio antes de escoger.**

| English: | I should stay at home tonight because I have a test tomorrow. |
| Spanish: | **Debo quedarme en casa esta noche, porque mañana tengo un examen.** |

COMPOUND TENSES *(TIEMPOS COMPUESTOS)*

Present Perfect *(Perfecto)*

———————————— RULE ————————————

Formation: In Spanish, as in English, the compound tenses are formed by using the auxiliary or helping verb "to have" (*haber*) with past participles. The present perfect (*perfecto*) consists of the present tense of *haber* (*he, has, ha, hemos, habéis, han*) plus any past participle. The meaning is usually the same as in English: *he tomado*— I have taken, *he dicho*—I have said. This tense is sometimes used instead of the preterite to describe recent past actions. In such cases the English translation of the verb may be simple past. (*Han votado*— they voted; *he asistido*—I attended.)

Ha sido un hombre de acción y *ha ganado* el éxito.
He has been a man of action and (he) *has won* success.

Ya *has escrito* más de cien páginas.
You've already *written* more than a hundred pages.

Una etiqueta magnética *ha desencadenado* la alarma.
A magnetic tag *has set off* the alarm.

PITFALL

The English expression **"have just" + a past participle** is not translated into Spanish by the present perfect. The present of ***acabar* (to finish, end) + the infinitive of the verb** is required.

Acabamos de aterrizar en Barajas.
We have just landed at Barajas.

Se acaba de anunciar en la televisión que ha muerto la víctima.

It has just been announced on television that the victim has died.

PITFALL

Duration of time is not normally expressed by the present perfect progressive in Spanish. In such statements, the verb *hacer* is used with the present tense. (See section on Time Expressions for a detailed presentation.)

English:	She has been talking on the phone for more than an hour.
Spanish:	**Hace más de una hora que está charlando por teléfono.**

Pluperfect and Preterite Perfect
(Pluscuamperfecto and Pretérito Perfecto)

Since there are two simple past tenses in Spanish, there are also two past perfect tenses—whereas English has only one. However, *the* **pluperfect** *is the commonly used tense and the* **preterite perfect** *is relatively rare.* (Specifically, it is used after conjunctions of time—*así que, en cuanto, tan pronto como, después que, cuando, etc.* In nonliterary Spanish the simple preterite may be used in place of the preterite perfect.)

——————————— RULE ———————————
Formation: The **pluperfect** is formed by the imperfect of *haber* (*había, habías, había, habíamos, habíais, habían*) plus a past participle.

——————————— RULE ———————————
Formation: The **preterite perfect** is formed by the preterite of *haber* (*hube, hubiste, hubo, hubimos, hubisteis, hubieron*) plus a past participle.

Esta mañana supimos que *había bajado* la Bolsa.
This morning we learned that the Stock Market *had declined.*

Cuando llegamos, ya *habían cerrado* la puerta con llave.
When we got there, they *had* already *locked* the door.

Tan pronto como *hubo leído* la noticia, me mandó un telegrama (or: **Tan pronto como leyó la noticia. . .**)
As soon as *he had read* the news, he sent me a telegram.

PITFALL

The English expression **"had just" + a past participle** is not translated into Spanish by the pluperfect nor by the preterite perfect. The imperfect of ***acabar* (to finish, end) + the infinitive of the verb** is required.

El avión *acababa de aterrizar*
The airplane *had just landed.*

PITFALL

Duration of time in the past is not normally expressed by the past perfect progressive in Spanish. In such statements, the verb *hacer* is used with the imperfect tense (See section on Time Expressions for a detailed presentation.)

English: I *had been studying* for a few minutes when I fell asleep.
Spanish: **Hacía unos pocos minutos que *estudiaba* cuando me dormí.**

Future Perfect *(Futuro Perfecto)*

—————————— RULE ——————————

Formation: The future perfect tense may be translated by the English future perfect. It is formed by the future of *haber (habré, habrás, habrá, habremos, habréis, habrán)* plus a past participle.

Para 2005 *habremos leído* todas las novelas de Galdós.
By 2005 *we shall have read* all the novels of Galdós.

PITFALL

Since the future is used to express probability in Spanish, the future perfect has a similar function to express probability or conjecture in the recent past.

¿A quién habrán invitado?
Whom do you suppose they've invited?

Conditional Perfect *(Condicional Perfecto)*

――――――――――――― RULE ―――――――――――――

Formation: The conditional perfect in Spanish is like the comparable English tense. It is formed by the conditional of *haber* (*habría, habrías, habría, habríamos, habríais, habrían*) plus a past participle.

――――――――――――――――――――――――――――――――――

Si hubiera sabido la verdad, la *habría ayudado*.
If I had known the truth, *I would have helped* her.

***No habrían podido* hacer el viaje en enero.**
They would not have been able to make the trip in January.

PITFALL

Again the expression of probability or conjecture in the past is a use to be noted carefully in order to avoid an incorrect reading.

***Habrían sido* las dos cuando me acosté.**
It must have been two o'clock when I went to bed.

¿Qué *habrían dicho*?
I wonder what they could have said.

THE SUBJUNCTIVE AND ITS TENSES

For the English-speaking student of Spanish, the most troublesome aspect of the Spanish verb is the subjunctive. Although English speakers use the subjunctive daily—generally without even being aware that they're doing so—this mood of the verb has been replaced by substitute forms in many instances. A few examples from recent American newspaper articles and editorials will illustrate the presence of the subjunctive in contemporary English:

> "We wish it *weren't so,* but we have the feeling of witnessing . . . a carefully planned performance."

> (Try substituting "wasn't" for "weren't" to test your feeling for the subjunctive.)

> "It is imperative that the Secretary of Transportation *come* forward with a more comprehensive design."

> (Again substitute the indicative -comes- for the subjunctive verb and try reading the sentence.)

> "The report recommends that the walls of the capitol *be* maintained and repaired."

> (If still in doubt, try "are" in this sentence.)

> "The C.A.B. eliminated the "affinity" rule that chartering groups *be* organized for a purpose other than air travel."

PITFALL

Because of the sameness of English verb forms, the subjunctive is apparent only in the 3rd person singular of the present subjunctive (which does not have the final "s") and in the present and past subjunctive forms of the verb "to be." Subjunctive ideas are expressed most commonly with the auxiliaries "may" and "might."

> "It's possible that we may go to Europe."

"Although he may be telling the truth, he speaks unconvincingly."

"I thought that they might call us."

In modern Spanish there are four subjunctive tenses: present subjunctive (*presente del subjuntivo*), imperfect subjunctive (*imperfecto del subjuntivo*), present perfect subjunctive (*perfecto del subjuntivo*), and pluperfect subjunctive (*pluscuamperfecto del subjuntivo*).

Subjunctive Tenses

Present	hable	**Es (una) lástima que *hable* tanto.** It's a shame *he talks* so much.
Imperfect	hablara/ hablase	**Dudaban que *habláramos* español.** They doubted that *we spoke* Spanish.
Present Perfect	haya hablado	**Es bueno que ellos *hayan hablado* bien.** It's good that *they have spoken* well.
Pluperfect	hubiera hablado/ hubiese hablado	**Ojalá ellos no *hubieran hablado* tanto.** I wish *they had* not *talked* so much.

Subjunctive Formation

—————————————————— RULE ——————————————————

The **present subjunctive** of -*ar* verbs is formed by adding the endings -*e, -es, -e, -emos, -éis, en* to the stem of the verb; the endings -*a, -as, -a, -amos -áis, -an* are added to the stems of -*er* and -*ir* verbs. The present subjunctive of most irregular verbs is based on the 1st person present indicative:

tener:—tengo—tenga
venir:—vengo—venga
decir:—digo—diga
conocer:—conozco
 —conozca

(*Exceptions:* dar, estar, haber, ir, saber, ser)

and others

RULE

The **present perfect subjunctive** is composed of the present subjunctive of *haber (haya, hayas, haya, hayamos, hayáis, hayan)* plus the past participle of the verb. *(haya tomado, haya dicho, etc.)*

RULE

The **imperfect subjunctive** has two forms. The "*ra*" form is obtained by removing the final "*ron*" from the 3rd person plural of the preterite of any Spanish verb and adding the endings *-ra, -ras, ra, -ramos, -rais, -ran*. The "*se*" form is derived from the same 3rd person plural preterite stem and the endings *-se, -ses, -se, -semos, -seis, -sen* are added.

---

toma	ron	tomara, tomase
vendie	ron	vendiera, vendiese
salie	ron	saliera, saliese
dije	ron	dijera, dijese

PITFALL

In the first person plural of both imperfect subjunctive forms, an accent is added to the final vowel of the preterite stem *(tomáramos, vendiésemos, dijéramos, etc.)*

RULE

The **pluperfect subjunctive** consists of either the "*ra*" or the "*se*" form of the imperfect subjunctive of the verb *haber (hubiera, hubieras, etc. or hubiese, hubieses, etc.)* plus the past participle of the verb. *(hubiera tomado, hubiese dicho, etc.)*

Sequence of Tenses

Since a subjunctive verb generally occurs in a dependent clause and is used in conjunction with a main indicative verb, care must be paid to correctness of tense sequences (or agreement). Only specific combinations are permitted. For example, a present subjunctive is normally not dependent on a main verb which is in a past tense (although there are exceptions). It is helpful to remember that the most common sequence in everyday speech is *present indicative* followed by *present subjunctive*; and that the past tenses, with the exception of the *present* perfect, are almost always followed by an *imperfect* or *pluperfect* subjunctive. The following chart illustrates the most expected sequences:

COMMON SEQUENCES

Indicative Tense of Main Verb	Subjunctive Tenses Permissible in Dependent Clause
Present Future Imperatives (Commands) Present Perfect Future Perfect	Present Subjunctive or Present Perfect Subjunctive (occasionally, Imperfect Subjunctive)

Indicative Tense of Main Verb	Subjunctive Tenses Permissible in Dependent Clause
Imperfect Preterite Conditional Pluperfect Conditional Perfect	Imperfect Subjunctive or Pluperfect Subjunctive

EXAMPLES:

Present Indicative : Present Subjunctive
Espero que *lleguen* a tiempo.
I hope (that) they'll arrive on time.

Command : Present Subjunctive
Diles que *lleguen* a tiempo.
Tell them to arrive on time.

Present Indicative : Present Perfect Subjunctive
Espero que *hayan llegado* a tiempo.
I hope they've arrived on time.

Imperfect Indicative : Imperfect Subjunctive
Esperaba que *llegaran* a tiempo.
I was hoping that they arrived on time.

Imperfect Indicative : Pluperfect Subjunctive
Esperaba que *hubieran llegado* a tiempo.
I was hoping that they had arrived on time.

PITFALL

A main verb in a past tense can never be followed by a verb in the present subjunctive. A past subjunctive is required.

Incorrect Spanish: **Dudaban que la función *empiece* a las 10.30.**
Correct Spanish: **Dudaban que la función *empezase (empe-zara)* a las 10.30.**

Uses of the Subjunctive
It should be remembered that the subjunctive represents the attitude of a person toward another person, thing, or action. Although the subjunctive verb is usually fixed and required by the nature of an introductory or principal clause, on occasion its use may be the subjective choice of the speaker. The subjunctive could also be considered to be "triggered" by a mental reaction, an emotion, a denial, or an uncer-

tainty. An important step toward mastery of the subjunctive is in acquiring a familiarity with certain words (verbs, conjunctions, and expressions) that invariably serve as subjunctive "triggers."

SUBJUNCTIVE IN NOUN CLAUSES

─────────────── RULE ───────────────

Formation: A **noun clause** is a group of words with a subject and a predicate that has the same relation to a verb (or preposition) that a noun would have. Such a clause is introduced by **que**. When the subjunctive rather than the indicative is used in a noun clause, the subjects of the verb in the main clause and that of the verb in the dependent noun clause must be different, and the verb must contain an idea that requires a following subjunctive.

	Main Verb	*Dependent Verb*
Indicative:	**Yo *sé* que ella *tiene* la culpa.**	
	(I know that she is to blame.)	

	Main Verb	*Dependent Verb*
Subjunctive:	***Dudo* que ella *tenga* la culpa.**	
	(I doubt that she is to blame.)	

	Introductory expression	*Dependent Verb*
Subjunctive:	**No *era posible* que *volviesen* a tiempo.**	
	(It was not possible that they would return on time.)	

─────────────── RULE ───────────────

In noun clauses the subjunctive is used after verbs that express emotion, mental action or attitude, or negation. Among the most common are: *querer* (to wish, want), *desear* (to want), *esperar* (to hope), *dudar* (to doubt), *temer* (to fear), *tener miedo de* (to fear), *negar* (to deny), *alegrarse de* (to be happy about), *gustar* (to like), *sentir* (to regret) and *no creer* (not to believe).

No quiero que salgas.
I don't want you to leave.
(Literally: ". . . that you leave.")

No creíamos que hubiera escrito la carta.
We didn't believe that he had written the letter.

Espero que vuelvan pronto.
I hope (that) they'll come back soon.

PITFALL

The English verb "want" is frequently followed by an infinitive phrase. In Spanish the dependent infinitive is possible only when there is no change of subject. Otherwise a subjunctive clause is mandatory.

	(No change of subject)
English:	He wants to know the truth.
CORRECT SPANISH:	*Quiere saber la verdad.*
	(Change of subject)
English:	He wants me to tell the truth
INCORRECT SPANISH:	**Me quiere decir la verdad.**
CORRECT SPANISH:	*Quiere que yo diga la verdad.*

--- RULE ---

The subjunctive is also used in noun clauses that follow verbs that advise, suggest, show preference, give permission, prohibit, consent, and that show approval or disapproval. Common examples are: *pedir* (to ask), *rogar* (to beg), *decir* (to tell to do something), *aconsejar* (to advise), *sugerir* (to suggest), *permitir* (to permit), *dejar* (to let), *consentir* (to consent).

Le pidió que la ayudase.
She asked him to help her.
(Literally: ". . . that he might help her.")

¿Consiente su madre en que vaya por avión?
Does her mother consent to her going by plane?
(Literally: ". . . in that she go by plane?")

PITFALL

However, an infinitive is also permitted after *dejar, hacer, impedir, mandar,* and *permitir.*

Su madre no les permite jugar en la calle.
Their mother doesn't permit them to play in the street.

PITFALL

When the verb *decir* is used to convey an order, the subjunctive is required in the dependent clause. When it is used simply to convey information, the indicative follows.

Command: (Subjunctive)	**Le dije que dejara de fumar.** I told him to stop smoking.
Information conveyed: (Indicative)	**Me dijo que había dejado de fumar.** He told me that he had stopped smoking.
Command: (Subjunctive)	**¡Dígales que vuelvan en seguida!** Tell them to come back at once!
Information conveyed: (Indicative)	**Les diré que usted ha vuelto.** I'll tell them that you have returned.

—————————————— RULE ——————————————

The subjunctive is also used in noun clauses following impersonal verbs and impersonal expression with *ser.* Common examples are:

importar (to be important), *ser posible* (to be possible), *ser (una) lástima* (to be a pity), *ser necesario* (to be necessary), *no ser cierto* (not to be certain), *ser dudoso* (to be doubtful), *convenir* (to be to one's interest).

Importa que compre usted esta pintura.
It is important that you buy this painting.

Era lástima que no pudiera ir con nosotros.
It was a pity that he couldn't go with us.

Es dudoso que Carlos se quede en Guadalajara.
It's doubtful that Charles will remain in Guadalajara.

PITFALL

Several impersonal expressions are followed by the indicative because they contain an idea of certainty. However, when used negatively, these expressions require that a dependent verb be in the subjunctive.

ser verdad (to be true)   **ser claro** (to be clear)
ser cierto (to be certain)   **ser evidente** (to be evident)
                                 ser seguro (to be sure)

Es verdad que Miss Smith se ha casado con un torero, pero no es cierto que se hayan ido a Mallorca.
It's true that Miss Smith has married a bullfighter, but it's not certain that they've gone off to Mayorca

Es evidente que lo comprendes, pero no es evidente que hayas estudiado.
It's evident that you understand it, but it's not evident that you have studied.

PITFALL

Sometimes the main clause is omitted in an indirect command, and the subjunctive clause stands alone. However, the main verb is still sensed by the speaker and the listener.

¡Que me escuches!	=	**¡Quiero que me escuches!**
(Listen to me!)		(I want you to listen to me!)
¡Que lo haga Luis!	=	**¡Deje que lo haga Luis!**
(Let Louis do it!)		(Let Louis do it!)

SUBJUNCTIVE IN ADJECTIVE CLAUSES

──────────────── RULE ────────────────

Formation: An adjective clause modifies a noun or pronoun that is contained in the main clause. Adjective clauses in Spanish are commonly introduced by the relatives *que*, *quien*, and *quienes*. The subjunctive is required in adjective clauses when the antecedent is indefinite (whether person, place, or thing); when the antecedent is negative; and after the words *cualquiera* and *cualesquiera* (whichever), *quienquiera* and *quienesquiera* (whoever). (Note: *cualquiera* and *cualesquiera* drop the final *a* when they directly precede a noun.)

────────────────────────────────────

Definite:	**Tengo una camisa que costó veinte dólares.**
(Indicative)	I have a shirt that cost twenty dollars.
Indefinite:	**Busco una camisa que no cueste tanto.**
(Subjunctive)	I'm looking for a shirt that doesn't cost so much. (In the first example, the shirt is already in the possession of the speaker; in the second sentence, the shirt has yet to be identified.)
Definite:	**Viven en una casa que compraron en 1987.**
(Indicative)	The live in a house that they bought in 1987.
Indefinite:	**Querían comprar una casa que no estuviera tan lejos de la universidad.**
(Subjunctive)	They wanted to buy a house that wouldn't be so far from the university. (In the first example, the house was purchased and inhabited; in the second sentence there is no indication as to whether the house was found or not)

| Definite: | **Conozco a un señor que habla italiano.** |
| (Indicative) | I know a gentleman who speaks Italian. |

| Indefinite: | **¿Conoces a alguien que hable árabe?** |
| (Subjunctive) | Do you know anyone who speaks Arabic? |

| Negative: | **No hay nadie que sepa cuánto ha sufrido.** |
| (Subjunctive) | There's no one who knows how much she has suffered. |

Indefinite:	**Quienquiera que se atreva a hacer el papel**
(Subjunctive)	**de don Juan Tenorio tiene que ser buen actor.**
	Whoever dares to play the role of Don Juan Tenorio has to be a fine actor.

Cualquier fecha que me indiques será conveniente.
Whatever date you indicate will be suitable.

SUBJUNCTIVE IN ADVERB CLAUSES

─────────────────────── RULE ───────────────────────

Formation: An **adverbial clause** has the function of an adverb in relation to the main verb of the principal clause. The subjunctive is used in adverbial clauses when the action of the dependent clause is incomplete, indefinite, or unproved from the point of view of the speaker; and the indicative is required when the action is completed or factual. Such clauses are always introduced by a conjunction of time, purpose, supposition, or concession. In short, the introductory word (or words) provides a first clue to appropriate usage.

Conjunctions Followed by Either Subjunctive or Indicative

cuando	when, whenever
después que	after
hasta que	until
aunque	although, even though, even if
mientras	while, as long as

en cuanto	as soon as
tan pronto como	as soon as
luego que	as soon as
así que	as soon as
de manera que	so as, so that
de modo que	so that
a pesar de que	in spite of the fact that
siempre que	provided that, whenever
porque	because, so that
como	since, as

Indicative: **Cuando mi avión aterrizó, un coche me estaba esperando.**
When my plane landed, a car was waiting for me.
(Action in the dependent clause is completed and factual.)

Subjunctive: **Cuando su avión aterrice, un coche le estará esperando.**
When(ever) your plane lands, a car will be waiting for you.
(Action in the dependent clause is incomplete.)

Subjunctive: **Me dijeron que un coche me estaría esperando cuando aterrizase el avión.**
They told me that a car would be waiting for me when the plane landed.
(Although the statement was made in the past, the action was still incomplete in relation to the main verb.)

Indicative: **El piloto esperó hasta que le dieron la señal.**
The pilot waited until they gave him the signal.
(completed action)

Subjunctive: **El piloto debe esperar hasta que le den la señal.**
The pilot must wait until they give him the signal.
(incomplete action)

Indicative: **Aunque ha recibido el bachillerato, no sabe nada de la física ni de la astronomía.**
Although he has received his secondary school diploma, he knows nothing about physics or astronomy.
(the dependent clause concedes an unquestionable fact.)

Subjunctive: **Aunque todavía no sepa nada de la astronomía, estudia para ser astronauta.**
Although he still doesn't know anything about astronomy, he is studying to be an astronaut.
(Here the dependent clause concedes a situation that is not finalized and which is subject to other opinions.)

Conjunctions Always Followed by Subjunctive

como si	as if
sin que	without
antes (de) que	before
para que	in order that
a menos que	unless
a no ser que	unless
a fin de que	in order that
con tal que	provided that
en caso de que	in case that, supposing that

Le escribí para que supiera mi dirección nueva.
I wrote to him so that he would (might) know my new address.

Espero cenar con ellos antes que se marchen.
I hope to have dinner with them before they leave.

Conjunctions Used Always with Indicative

puesto que	since, inasmuch as
mientras que	whereas

Verbs

| ya que | since, now that |
| ahora que | now that |

SUBJUNCTIVE IN CONDITIONS CONTRARY TO FACT ("IF" CLAUSES)

———————————————— RULE ————————————————

Formation: The **imperfect** or **pluperfect subjunctive** is used in a clause introduced by **si** (if) to express a condition contrary to fact or to express a hypothesis. The related result clause will be in the conditional or conditional perfect—or the "ra" forms of the imperfect and pluperfect subjunctive may be substituted for conditional and conditional perfect respectively.

Contrary to Fact:	**Si mi hermano estuviera aquí, se enamoraría (enamorara) de esa chica.** If my brother were here, he'd fall in love with that girl.
	Si mis padres hubieran llegado ayer, habríamos (hubiéramos) podido ir a Toledo esta tarde. If my parents had arrived yesterday, we would have been able to go to Toledo this afternoon.
Hypothesis:	**Si fuese a España en mayo, podría (pudiera) ver a mis amigos en la universidad.** If I were to go to Spain in May, I'd be able to see my friends at the university.

PITFALL

The **present subjunctive** is *never* used in a clause introduced by *si*. When the English verb is in the present in an "if" clause, the Spanish verb will be present indicative.

Si voy al cine esta noche, no leeré esa novela de Matute.
If I go to the movies tonight, I won't read that novel by Matute.

SUBJUNCTIVE WITH *OJALÁ*

The introductory word *ojalá* is derived from the Arabic *in shá llah* (Allah grant . . .) and has the meaning in Spanish of "I hope that" or "Would that." It is always followed by the subjunctive.

Ojalá que ganen el premio.
I hope they'll win the prize.

Ojalá que hubieran ganado el premio.
I wish that they had won the prize.

COMMANDS *(MANDATOS)*

Spanish commands take into consideration the four words for you: *tú, vosotros (as), usted,* and *ustedes*; but the only "true imperatives" are the affirmative forms for *tú* and *vosotros*. The affirmative command forms for *usted* and *ustedes*, and all the negative commands, are derived from the present subjunctive tense.

Formation of Commands

AFFIRMATIVE	NEGATIVE
tú—Like 3rd. per. singular of present indicative tense, except for certain irregular forms. **canta, vende,** etc.	Same as 2nd person singular of present subjunctive. **no cantes, no vendas, no digas,** etc.
vosotros—Same as infinitive with *d* substituted for final *r*. **cantad, vended, decid,** etc.	Same as 2nd person plural of present subjunctive. **no cantéis, no vendáis no digáis,** etc.

usted—Same as 3rd person singular of present subjunctive. **cante (usted), diga (usted),** etc.	Same as 3rd person singular of present subjunctive. **no cante (usted), no diga (usted),** etc.
ustedes—Same as 3rd person plural of present subjunctive. **canten (ustedes)** etc.	Same as 3rd person plural of present subjunctive. **no canten (ustedes)** etc.

PITFALL

Object pronouns follow all affirmative commands and are attached to the end of the verb. The object pronouns precede the command if it is negative.

Affirmative: **Llámame mañana, Pablo.**
Call me tomorrow, Paul.

Miradnos, niños.
Look at us, children.

Dígamelo (usted), señor.
Tell it to me, sir.

Negative: **No me llames mañana, Pablo.**
Don't call me tomorrow, Paul.

No nos miréis, niños.
Don't look at us, children.

No me lo diga (usted), señor.
Don't tell it to me, sir.

PITFALL

When the reflexive *os* is added to the *vosotros* command, the final *d* of the verb is dropped (except for the verb *ir* [*idos*]). In the case of *-ir* verbs an accent is added to the final *i*.

Acostaos, niños. (Acostad + os)
Go to bed, children.

Poneos el sombrero. (Poned + os)
Put on your hats.

Vestíos. (Vestid + os)
Get dressed.

PITFALL

When using reflexive verbs it is essential that the reflexive pronoun correspond to the command form that is employed.

INCORRECT SPANISH: **Acuéstase.**
Divertidse.
Levántete.

CORRECT SPANISH: *Acuéstate.*
Divertíos.
Levántese.

PITFALL

A small group of common verbs have irregular affirmative familiar (tú) command forms.

tener—ten (have)	**salir—sal** (leave)
hacer—haz (do)	**ser—sé** (be)
poner—pon (put)	**decir—di** (say, tell)
venir—ven (come)	**ir—ve** (go)

THE INFINITIVE

In English, the infinitive has no identifying ending, but it is usually accompanied by the preposition *to* (to spend, to eat, to receive). In Spanish, the form is immediately recognizable by the endings *-ar*, *-er*, *-ir (gastar, comer, recibir)*. While some Spanish verbs require a particular preposition—most frequently *a* or *de*—before a dependent infinitive [See section on Prepositions for lists], many other common verbs take a direct infinitive.

> **Quería comprar una calculadora de bolsillo.**
> (Never: **"Quería a comprar"**)
> *I wanted to buy* a pocket calculator.

> **Debemos telefonearla pronto.**
> *We ought to telephone* her soon.

> **Esperaban ver el "Guernica" en el Museo Reina Sofía.**
> *They were hoping to see* "Guernica" in the Reina Sofía Museum.

PITFALL

Some infinitives have become permanent nouns in the Spanish language and consequently function both as verbs and nouns.

deber to owe, ought	**el deber** duty
pesar to weigh	**el pesar** sorrow, regret
poder to be able, can	**el poder** power
ser to be	**el ser** being, essence

PITFALL

The infinitive is often used as a command or imperative on signs in public places.

No fumar	No Smoking
No escupir	No Spitting
No pisar	Keep Off

PITFALL

The infinitive after verbs such as *dejar*, *hacer*, and *mandar* often denotes a passive construction.

> **El lo hizo construir.**
> He had it built.

Mandarán abrir la cajita de seguridad.
They will order the safe-deposit box to be opened.

THE PRESENT PARTICIPLE *(EL GERUNDIO)*

─────────────── RULE ───────────────

Formation: The Spanish **present participle** is formed by adding *-ando* to the stem of *-ar* verbs and *-iendo* to the stems of *-er* and *-ir* verbs *(tomando, vendiendo, viviendo, etc.)*. Verbs ending in *-ir* that have a *-u* or *-i* stem change show the change in the present participle *(durmiendo, pidiendo, diciendo, etc.)*. The present participle of the verb *ir* (to go) is *yendo*.

─────────────── RULE ───────────────

The most common use of the present participle is to combine with the verb *estar* (NEVER *ser*) to form the progressive tenses.

Juan está mirando las estrellas.
John is looking at the stars.

Estábamos durmiendo en la playa.
We were sleeping on the beach.

─────────────── RULE ───────────────

The present participle is also used in a progressive sense with the verbs *ir*, *venir*, *andar*, *seguir*, and *continuar*.

Los estudiantes iban cantando por las calles.
The students went singing through the streets.

El profesor seguía hablando aunque los estudiantes estaban dormidos.
The teacher kept on talking even though the students were asleep.

PITFALL

The Spanish present participle—although called the *gerundio*— is not the equivalent of the English gerund. The *gerundio* may not be used as a noun (or as an adjective) in Spanish. The English gerund is normally translated into Spanish with an infinitive.

English:	Seeing is believing.
INCORRECT SPANISH:	**Viendo es creyendo.**
CORRECT SPANISH:	*Ver es creer.*
English:	My father says that creating fantasies is not worth the trouble.
INCORRECT SPANISH:	**Mi padre dice que creando fantasías no vale la pena.**
CORRECT SPANISH:	*Mi padre dice que el crear fantasías no vale la pena.* (or: *. . . no vale la pena crear fantasías.*)

THE PAST PARTICIPLE *(EL PARTICIPIO)*

———————————— RULE ————————————

Formation: **Past participles** are formed by adding *-ado* to the infinitive stem of *-ar* verbs and *-ido* to the stems of *-er* and *-ir* verbs.

———————————————————————————————

A group of common Spanish verbs (and their compounds) have irregular past participles:

abrir	**abierto** (opened)
decir	**dicho** (said, told)
escribir	**escrito** (written)
hacer	**hecho** (done, made)
morir	**muerto** (dead)
poner	**puesto** (put)
ver	**visto** (seen)
volver	**vuelto** (returned)

--- RULE ---

The basic function of the past participle is in the formation of the perfect tenses with the auxiliary verb *haber*. It is also used with *ser* to express the passive voice, and with *estar* and *quedar(se)* to express the result of an action. Many past participles also function as pure adjectives and show agreement in gender and number with the nouns they modify.

Me *había escrito* muchas cartas.
He *had written* me many letters.

¿Quién *ha dicho* tal cosa?
Who *has said* such a thing?

La puerta *fue abierta* por la policía.
The door *was opened* by the police.

La puerta *está abierta*; no sé quién la abrió.
The door *is open*; I don't know who opened it.

Es una actriz muy *conocida* en Cuba.
She is an actress well known in Cuba.

Al oír la confesión, sus padres se quedaron *aturdidos*.
When his parents heard the confession, they were (left) stunned.

THE PASSIVE VOICE *(LA VOZ PASIVA)*

--- RULE ---

Formation: *A verb form changes from active to passive when the verb acts upon the subject, rather than an object, by means of an agent (expressed or implied).* In English the passive voice is formed with the verb "to be" and the past participle of a transitive verb. In Spanish the verb *ser* is used to translate "to be" and the past participle agrees in number and gender with the subject. Unlike most Spanish constructions, the *true* passive may be successfully translated word for word into English in a direct declarative sentence. (However, this would not hold true for questions.)

| Spanish: | **El aire *ha sido* contaminado por los automóviles.** |
| English: | The air *has been contaminated* by the automobiles. |

| Spanish: | **La enfermedad fue provocada por la radioactividad.** |
| English: | The sickness *was caused* by radioactivity. |

But

| Spanish: | **¿Cuándo *será explicada* esta lección?** |
| English: | When *will* this lesson *be explained*? |

The "False" Passive

In English the verb "to be" is frequently used with the past participle to express the result *of a previous action rather than the action itself. This is sometimes called the* "**false**" *or* "**pseudo**" **passive** (for lack of a better name) because it may *appear* to be a passive construction when out of context.

> For example: "The door is closed."
>
> Is it being closed now or is it already firmly closed as the result of someone's having closed it earlier? In English we do not know which is intended unless an agent is expressed or some qualifying phrase is added: "The door is closed by the guard." (True passive); 'The door is closed and I don't have a key." (False passive)

PITFALL

In Spanish there is no confusion since ***ser* + a past participle** is used for the passive voice, and ***estar* + a past participle** indicates the result of a previous action. The pitfall for the English-speaking students lies in transferring the ambiguity of his own language to Spanish. It is sometimes helpful to remember that the Spanish verb *estar* comes from the Latin verb *stare* (to stand) and that it describes a state or condition.

La puerta está cerrada. (The door is closed.)
The door "stands" closed.

    or

(The door is closed because someone closed it earlier.)

Mi hermano está disgustado.
My brother is displeased. (because something displeased him
earlier.)

El ejército estaba derrotado.
The army was defeated. (**porque había sido derrotado antes
por el enemigo.**)

PITFALL

Whenever an agent is given, the sentence is clearly *true* passive and
must be rendered accordingly:

La ciudad es amenazada por la contaminación atmosférica.
The city is threatened by air pollution.

The Reflexive *se* Substitute for the Passive Voice

One of the most characteristic constructions of the Spanish language
is the favored use of a reflexive construction as a substitute for the
true passive when no agent is expressed. English has no exact grammatical equivalent, although such constructions are frequently translated by "one" or an indefinite "they" plus an active verb.

Aquí se habla español.
Spanish (is) spoken here.
(but literally: Spanish speaks itself here.)

No se usa "usted" entre amigos.
"*Usted*" isn't used among friends.

    or

One doesn't use "usted" among friends.
(but literally: "*Usted*" doesn't use itself among friends.)

Se admitían tarjetas de crédito en esta librería.
Credit cards used to be accepted in this bookstore.
> or
They used to accept credit cards in this bookstore.
(but literally: Credit cards used to accept themselves. . .)

PITFALL

It must be remembered that even when *se* is translated into English by "one" or "they," the Spanish verb agrees with its Spanish subject in number and not with the words used in translation. Consequently:

One can buy postcards here.
Se pueden comprar tarjetas postales aquí.
(the subject, *tarjetas,* is plural and the verb *pueden* agrees.)

They say that he is going to receive the Nobel Prize.
Se dice que va a recibir el Premio Nobel.
(the subject—the clause introduced by *que*—is singular and requires that *dice* be singular.)

PITFALL

When the *se* construction is used with a person rather than a thing, the verb is *always* 3rd person singular and the English subject becomes the object of the Spanish verb.

Se les veía en Madrid.
They were seen in Madrid.
> or
Someone saw them in Madrid.
("Se veían en Madrid" would mean "They used to see each other in Madrid.)

Se le invitó a Carlos.
Charles was invited.

REFLEXIVE VERBS

It should be remembered that reflexive verbs are more common in Spanish than in English and that frequently a Spanish reflexive form cannot be translated by an English reflexive (also see section on Reflexive Pronouns).

Spanish	English
acostarse	to go to bed
levantarse	to get up
sentarse	to sit down
sentirse	to feel
ponerse	to put on
despedirse	to take leave of, say goodbye to
divertirse	to have a good time
enamorarse	to fall in love
hacerse	to become
and many others	

PITFALL

Frequently a Spanish reflexive verb will be expressed in English by *to get* or *to become*.

Después de volver a casa, se enfermaron de la gastritis.
After returning home, they got sick with gastritis.

No creo que te aburras durante la función.
I don't believe you'll get (become) bored during the performance.

Se ha enriquecido porque hizo muchas inversiones.
He has become rich because he made many investments.

PITFALL

Many common reflexive verbs may also be used in Spanish in a non-reflexive sense.

> **Me acosté a las once.**
> I went to bed at eleven
>> But
> **Acosté al niño a las once.**
> I put the child to bed at eleven.
>
> **Nos lavamos las manos.**
> We washed our hands.
>> But
> **Le lavamos la cara al niño.**
> We washed the child's face.

PITFALL

Some verbs are used both reflexively and non-reflexively but with different meanings.

acordar to agree to	**acordarse** to remember
burlar to mock, deceive	**burlarse** to make fun of
decidir to decide	**decidirse** to make up one's mind
detener to detain	**detenerse** to stop
dirigir to direct	**dirigirse** to address
dormir to sleep	**dormirse** to go to sleep
encontrar to meet	**encontrarse** to be situated, located
llamar to call	**llamarse** to be named
negar to deny	**negarse** to refuse
ocupar to occupy	**ocuparse** to be busy with
parecer to seem, appear	**parecerse** to resemble
poner to put	**ponerse** to put on, to begin to
volver to return	**volverse** to turn around

VERBS OF OBLIGATION

English obligation is expressed by "must," "ought," "should," "have to," "to be to," and "to be supposed to." "Must," "ought," and "should" are defective verbs (*i.e.* they exist only in certain tenses), but their Spanish equivalents are complete and may be expressed in all tenses. The common verbs of obligation in Spanish are *tener que*, *deber*, and *haber de*.

────────────── RULE ──────────────

Tener que indicates compulsion, generally of an outward nature.

> **Tengo que estudiar porque mañana hay examen en física.**
> *I have to (must) study* because tomorrow there's a test in Physics.

> **Tendremos que salir antes de las siete.**
> *We'll have to (we must) leave* before seven.
> (because we have to catch a plane at eight)

────────────── RULE ──────────────

Deber generally indicates moral obligation.

> **Debes (or debieras) continuar tu carrera el año que viene.**
> *You should (ought to)* go on with your studies next year.
> (for the sake of all concerned)

> **Juan no debe (debiera) fumar tanto.**
> John *ought not (shouldn't)* smoke so much.

PITFALL

Note, however, that ***deber + de*** expresses probability and not obligation.

> **Debe de ser el piloto del avión.**
> *He must be* the pilot of the airplane.

PITFALL

Deber in the past must be translated by "ought" or "should" plus a perfect infinitive (to have + past participle).

> **Debieron acompañar a sus hijos.**
> They *should (ought) to have gone with* their children
>
> **Debiste continuar la carrera este año.**
> You *should (ought to) have gone on with* your studies this year.

—————————————— RULE ——————————————

Haber de indicates mild obligation translated into English by "to be to" or "to be supposed to."

> **He de asistir a una conferencia en Filadelfia.**
> *I'm supposed to attend* a lecture in Philadelphia.
>
> **Habíamos de mostrarles las películas que filmamos en Bogotá.**
> *We were (supposed) to show* them the films we made in Bogotá.

PITFALL

Hay que (había que, hubo que, etc.) is an impersonal expression of obligation. It can never be used when referring to a specific person.

> **Hay que soñar para vivir.**
> One must dream in order to live.
>
> **No hay que dedicar tanto tiempo a los toros.**
> One shouldn't devote so much time to the bullfights.

SER VERSUS *ESTAR*

Since both *ser* and *estar* are translated by the English verb "to be," they create pitfalls for the English-speaking student.

----------------------- RULE -----------------------

Ser, from the Latin verb *esse* (to be) is used to indicate origin, possession, material, and to tell time. When the word following "to be" is a noun or pronoun, *ser* is also required. With terms of nationality, religion, political affiliation, and profession *ser* is appropriate.

El chico que acaba de llegar *es* de Alemania. Su padre *es* médico y su madre *es* una abogada española.

The boy who has just arrived *is* from Germany. His father *is* a doctor and his mother *is* a Spanish lawyer.

----------------------- RULE -----------------------

Ser is used with adjectives that denote basic qualities of physique, intellect, or personality. It is also used with adjectives indicating age.

Cuando el señor Gómez *era* joven, nadie sabía que *era tan* inteligente ni astuto.
When Señor Gómez *was* young, no one knew that he *was* so intelligent or clever.

Dolores *es* rubia, guapa y amable.
Dolores *is* blond, beautiful, and nice.

----------------------- RULE -----------------------

Estar, from the Latin *stare* (to stand), indicates location, an impermanent condition (as opposed to a physical characteristic) and states of being or nonbeing, regardless of permanence. It is also used with the present participle *(gerundio)* to form the progressive forms of the verb.

Mi primo *está* muy contento porque ha recibido su bachillerato.
My cousin *is* very happy because he has received his diploma.

***Estaba* enfermo y no podía ir a la presentación.**
He *was* sick and could not go to the presentation.

Ahora *está* estudiando más que nunca.
Now he is studying more than ever.

Ser describes something or someone that is characteristically that way.

El gazpacho es frío.
Gazpacho is cold. (That is, always served cold.)

Estar is often used to express the condition of the moment expressed by the English verbs *feel, look,* or *taste.*

Esta sopa está fría.
This soup is (tastes) cold.

Carmen está vieja.
Carmen looks old. (She is not old, however.)

Because *ser* + adjective expresses a characteristic and *estar* + *adjective* expresses a condition, many adjectives can be used with both verbs but with different meanings.

	With Ser	With Estar
abierto	frank	open
aburrido	boring	bored
alegre	happy (by nature)	happy (mood)
bajo	short	in a low position
bueno	good (by nature)	well (in good health)
callado	close-mouthed	silent
cierto	true	certain, assured
despierto	alert	awake
divertido	amusing	amused

enfermo	sickly	sick
listo	clever	ready
loco	crazy (by nature)	crazy (frantic)
malo	bad (by nature)	sick
seguro	safe, reliable	sure, positive
verde	green	unripe
vivo	lively	alive

PITFALL

The preposition *de* must be used in impersonal expressions when ***ser*** **+ adjective** is preceded by an expressed or implied subject. The sentence then has a passive force.

> **Esto es difícil de explicar.**
> This is difficult to explain.

> **Esa música es fácil de tocar.**
> That music is easy to play.

However, when the infinitive that follows *ser* is really its subject, the passive force is lost and *de* is omitted.

> **Es fácil tocar esa música.**
> It's easy to play that music.

(Note: For other uses of *ser* and *estar*, see section on the Passive Voice.)

RADICAL OR STEM-CHANGING VERBS

The stems of many Spanish verbs are subject to a vowel "split" when stressed, and some *-ir* verbs have an additional vowel change when the stem is followed by a stressed *a*, *ie*, or *io*.

PITFALL

Radical-changing verbs of the first and second conjugations (*ar* and *er* verbs) change stressed *e* to *ie,* and stressed *o* to *ue.* These changes occur *only* in the 1st, 2nd, and 3rd singular and the 3rd plural forms of the present indicative and present subjunctive. (The change cannot occur in other tenses because the stress is not on the stem but on the endings.)

Contar (to tell)

Pres. Ind.:   *cuento, cuentas, cuenta,* **contamos, contáis,** *cuentan*

Pres. Subj.:   *cuente, cuentes, cuente,* **contemos, contéis,** *cuenten*

Perder (to lose)

Pres. Ind.:   *pierdo, pierdes, pierde,* **perdemos, perdéis,** *pierden*

Pres. Subj.:   *pierda, pierdas, pierda,* **perdamos, perdáis,** *pierdan*

Note: The singular verb *jugar* (to play) has a change from *u* to *ue.*

PITFALL

Radical-Changing Verbs of the third conjugation (*ir* verbs) change a stressed *e* to *ie, e* to *i,* or *o* to *ue* in the same forms of the present indicative and present subjunctive as first and second conjugation verbs. They have additional changes of *e* to *i* and *o* to *u* in the 3rd singular and plural of the preterite, in all forms of the imperfect subjunctive, in the 1st and 2nd plural of the present subjunctive, and in the present participle.

Sentir (to feel, regret)

Pres. Ind.:   *siento, sientes, siente,* **sentimos, sentís,** *sienten*

Pres. Subj.:   *sienta, sientas, sienta, sintamos, sintáis, sientan*

Preterite:	**sentí sentiste,** *sintió,* **sentimos, sentisteis,** *sintieron*
Imp. Subj.:	*sintiera, sintieras,* etc.
	sintiese, sintieses, etc.
Pres. Part:	*sintiendo*

Pedir (to ask for)

Pres. Ind.:	*pido, pides, pide,* **pedimos, pedís,** *piden*
Pres. Subj.:	*pida, pidas, pida, pidamos, pidáis, pidan*
Preterite:	**pedí, pediste,** *pidió,* **pedimos, pedisteis,** *pidieron*
Imp. Subj.:	*pidiera, pidieras,* etc.
	pidiese, pidieses, etc.
Pres. Part.:	*pidiendo*

ORTHOGRAPHIC OR SPELLING-CHANGING VERBS

Many Spanish verbs undergo a spelling change in some tenses so that the pronunciation of the stem may remain consistent and the rules of spelling not be violated. Remember that the spelling must retain the sound of the infinitive in Spanish.

—————————————— RULE ——————————————

Verbs ending in *-car* change *c* to *qu* before *e*.

Sacar   To Take Out

Preterite	Present Subjunctive
saqué	**saque**
sacaste	**saques**
sacó	**saque**
etc.	**saquemos**
	saquéis
	saquen

RULE

Verbs ending in -*gar* change *g* to *gu* before *e*.

Pagar   To Pay

Preterite	Present Subjunctive
pagué	**pague**
pagaste	**pagues**
pagó	**pague**
etc.	**paguemos**
	paguéis
	paguen

RULE

Verbs ending in -*zar* change *z* to *c* before *e*.

Gozar   To Enjoy

Preterite	Present Subjunctive
gocé	**goce**
gozaste	**goces**
gozó	**goce**
etc.	**gocemos**
	gocéis
	gocen

RULE

Verbs ending in -*cer* or -*cir* preceded by a consonant change *c* to *z* before *o* and *a*.

Vencer   To Conquer

Present Indicative	Present Subjunctive
venzo	**venza**
vences	**venzas**

vence	**venza**
etc.	**venzamos**
	venzáis
	venzan

―――――――――――――― RULE ――――――――――――――

Verbs ending in *-ger* or *-gir* change *g* to *j* before *o* and *a*.

Coger   To Catch

Present Indicative	Present Subjunctive
cojo	**coja**
coges	**cojas**
coge	**coja**
etc.	**cojamos**
	cojáis
	cojan

Dirigir   To Direct

Present Indicative	Present Subjunctive
dirijo	**dirija**
diriges	**dirijas**
dirige	**dirija**
etc.	**dirijamos**
	dirijáis
	dirijan

―――――――――――――― RULE ――――――――――――――

Verbs ending in *-guir* change *gu* to *g* before *o* and *a*.

Distinguir   To Distinguish

Present Indicative	Present Subjunctive
distingo	**distinga**
distingues	**distingas**

distingue	**distinga**
etc.	**distingamos**
	distingáis
	distingan

--------------------------------- RULE ---------------------------------

Verbs ending in -*quir* change *qu* to *c* before *o* and *a*.

Delinquir   To Commit An Offense

Present Indicative   Present Subjunctive

delinco	**delinca**
delinques	**delincas**
delinque	**delinca**
etc.	**delincamos**
	delincáis
	delincan

--------------------------------- RULE ---------------------------------

Verbs ending in -*guar* change *gu* to *gü* before *e*.

Averiguar   To Ascertain

Preterite   Present Subjunctive

averigüé	**averigüe**
averiguaste	**averigües**
averiguó	**averigüe**
etc.	**averigüemos**
	averigüéis
	averigüen

RULE

Verbs ending in *-eer* change unstressed *i* to *y* between vowels.

Leer   To Read

Preterite	Imperfect Subjunctive		Participles: Present, Past
leí	leyera	leyese	leyendo
leíste	leyeras	leyeses	leído
leyó	leyera	leyese	
leímos	etc.	etc.	
leísteis			
leyeron			

RULE

Verbs ending in *-eír* are radical-changing verbs that lose one *i* in the third person of the preterite, imperfect subjunctive, and present participle.

Reír   To Laugh

Present Indicative	Preterite	Imperfect Subjunctive		Present Participle
río	reí	riera	riese	riendo
ríes	reíste	rieras	rieses	
ríe	rió	riera	riese	
reímos	reímos	etc.	etc.	
reís	reísteis			
ríen	rieron			

RULE

Verbs whose stem ends in *ll* or *ñ* drop the *i* of the diphthongs *ie* and *ió.*

Bullir   To Boil

Preterite	Imperfect Subjunctive		Present Participle
bullí	**bullera**	**bullese**	**bullendo**
bulliste	**bulleras**	**bulleses**	
bulló	**bullera**	**bullese**	
bullimos	etc.	etc.	
bullisteis			
bulleron			

Reñir   To Scold (Also Radical Changing)

Preterite	Imperfect Subjunctive		Present Participle
reñí	**riñera**	**riñese**	**riñendo**
reñiste	**riñeras**	**riñeses**	
riñó	**riñera**	**riñese**	
reñimos	etc.	etc.	
reñisteis			
riñeron			

COMMON IRREGULAR VERBS

(Only the tenses containing irregular forms are given. All other forms are completely regular.)

Common Irregular Verb Forms

---

andar	**to walk, go**
Preterite	anduve, anduviste, anduvo, anduvimos, anduvisteis, anduvieron

Imperfect Subjunctive (-ra) anduviera, anduvieras, anduviera, anduviéramos, anduvierais, anduvieran
(-se) anduviese, anduvieses, anduviese, anduviésemos, anduvieseis, anduviesen

caber   **to be contained in**
Present Indicative   quepo, cabes, cabe, cabemos, cabéis, caben
Preterite   cupe, cupiste, cupo, cupimos, cupisteis, cupieron
Future Conditional   cabré, cabrás, cabrá, cabremos, cabréis, cabrán
                            cabría, cabrías, cabría, cabríamos, cabríais, cabrían
Present Subjunctive   quepa, quepas, quepa, quepamos, quepáis, quepan
Imperfect Subjunctive   (-ra) cupiera, cupieras, cupiera, cupiéramos, cupierais, cupieran
                            (-se) cupiese, cupieses, cupiese, cupiésemos, cupieseis, cupiesen

caer   **to fall**
Present Indicative   caigo, caes, cae, caemos, caéis, caen
Preterite   caí, caíste, cayó, caímos, caísteis, cayeron
Present Subjunctive   caiga, caigas, caiga, caigamos, caigáis, caigan
Imperfect Subjunctive   (-ra) cayera, cayeras, cayera, cayéramos, cayerais, cayeran
                            (-se) cayese, cayeses, cayese, cayésemos, cayeseis, cayesen
Present Participle   cayendo
Past Participle   caído

conducir   **to drive, to conduct**
(other verbs ending in *-ducir* are conjugated like *conducir*)

Present Indicative   conduzco, conduces, conduce, conducimos, conducís, conducen
Preterite   conduje, condujiste, condujo, condujimos, condujisteis, condujeron
Present Subjunctive   conduzca, conduzcas, conduzca, conduzcamos, conduzcáis, conduzcan

Imperfect Subjunctive (-ra) condujera, condujeras, condujera, condujéramos, condujerais, condujeran
(-se) condujese, condujeses, condujese, condujésemos, condujeseis, condujesen

conocer   **to know**
(all verbs ending in a vowel + *cer* or *cir*, except *cocer, hacer, mecer,* and their compounds, are conjugated like *conocer*.)

Present Indicative   conozco, conoces, conoce, etc.
Present Subjunctive   conozca, conozcas, conozca, conozcamos, conozcáis, conozcan

dar   **to give**
Present Indicative   doy, das, da, damos, dais, dan

Preterite   di, diste, dio, dimos, disteis, dieron
Present Subjunctive   dé, des, dé, demos, deis, den

Imperfect Subjunctive (-ra) diera, dieras, diera, diéramos, dierais, dieran
(-se) diese, dieses, diese, diésemos, dieseis, diesen

decir   **to say, tell**
Present Indicative   digo, dices, dice, decimos, decís, dicen
Preterite   dije, dijiste, dijo, dijimos, dijisteis, dijeron
Future   diré, dirás, dirá, diremos, diréis, dirán
Conditional   diría, diriás, diría, diríamos, diríais, dirían
Present Subjunctive   diga, digas, diga, digamos, digáis, digan
Imperfect Subjunctive (-ra) dijera, dijeras, dijera, dijéramos, dijerais, dijeran
(-se) dijese, dijeses, dijese, dijésemos dijeseis, dijesen
Present Participle   diciendo
Past Participle   dicho
Imperative   di, decid

errar **to err**
Present Indicative yerro, yerras, yerra, erramos, erráis, yerran
Present Subjunctive yerre, yerres, yerre, erremos, erréis, yerren
Imperative yerra, errad

estar **to be**
Present Indicative estoy, estás, está, estamos, estáis, están
Preterite estuve, estuviste, estuvo, estuvimos, estuvisteis, estuvieron
Present Subjunctive esté, estés, esté, estemos, estéis, estén
Imperfect Subjunctive (-ra) estuviera, estuvieras, estuviera, estuviéramos, estuvierais, estuvieran
(-es) estuviese, estuvieses, estuviese, estuviésemos, estuvieseis, etuviesen
Imperative está, estad

haber **to have**
Present Indicative he, has, ha, hemos, habéis, han
Preterite hube, hubiste, hubo, hubimos, hubisteis, hubieron
Future habré, habrás, habrá, habremos, habréis, habrán
Conditional habría, habrías, habría, habríamos, habríais, habrían
Present Subjunctive haya, hayas, haya, hayamos, hayáis, hayan
Imperfect Subjunctive (-ra) hubiera, hubieras, hubiera, hubiéramos, hubierais, hubieran
(-se) hubiese, hubieses, hubiese, hubiésemos, hubieseis, hubiesen

hacer **to do, make**
Present Indicative hago, haces, hace, hacemos, hacéis, hacen
Preterite hice, hiciste, hizo, hicimos, hicisteis, hicieron
Future haré, harás, hará, haremos, haréis, harán
Conditional haría, harías, haría, haríamos, haríais, harían
Present Subjunctive haga, hagas, haga, hagamos, hagáis, hagan
Imperfect Subjunctive (-ra) hiciera, hicieras, hiciera, hiciéramos, hicierais, hicieran

	(-se) hiciese, hicieses, hiciese, hiciésemos, hicieseis, hiciesen
Past Participle	hecho
Imperative	haz, haced

huir — to flee

(All verbs ending in -*uir*, except those ending in -*guir* and -*quir*, are conjugated like *huir*.)

Present Indicative	huyo, huyes, huye, huimos, huís, huyen
Preterite	huí, huiste, huyó, huimos, huisteis, huyeron
Present Subjunctive	huya, huyas, huya, huyamos, huyáis, huyan
Imperfect Subjunctive	(-ra) huyera, huyeras, huyera, huyéramos, huyerais, huyeran
	(-se) huyese, huyeses, huyese, huyésemos, huyeseis, huyesen
Present Participle	huyendo
Imperative	huye, huid

ir — to go

Present Indicative	voy, vas, va, vamos, vais, van
Imperfect Indicative	iba, ibas, iba, íbamos, ibais, iban
Preterite	fui, fuiste, fue, fuimos, fuisteis, fueron
Present Subjunctive	vaya, vayas, vaya, vayamos, vayáis, vayan
Imperfect Subjunctive	(-ra) fuera, fueras, fuera, fuéramos, fuerais, fueran
	(-se) fuese, fueses, fuese, fuésemos, fueseis, fuesen
Present Participle	yendo
Imperative	ve, id

oír — to hear

Present Indicative	oigo, oyes, oye, oímos, oís, oyen
Preterite	oí, oíste, oyó, oímos, oísteis, oyeron
Present Subjunctive	oiga, oigas, oiga, oigamos, oigáis, oigan
Imperfect Subjunctive	(-ra) oyera, oyeras, oyera, oyéramos, oyerais, oyeran
	(-se) oyese, oyeses, oyese, oyésemos, oyeseis, oyesen

Present Participle	oyendo
Past Participle	oído
Imperative	oye, oíd

oler — **to smell**

Present Indicative	huelo, hueles, huele, olemos, oléis, huelen
Present Subjunctive	huela, huelas, huela, olamos, oláis, huelan
Imperative	huele, oled

poder — **to be able**

Present Indicative	puedo, puedes, puede, podemos, podéis, pueden
Preterite	pude, pudiste, pudo, pudimos, pudisteis, pudieron
Future	podré, podrás, podrá, podremos, podréis, podrán
Conditional	podría, podrías, podría, podríamos, podríais, podrían
Present Subjunctive	pueda, puedas, pueda, podamos, podáis, puedan
Imperfect Subjunctive	(-ra) pudiera, pudieras, pudiera, pudiéramos, pudierais, pudieran
	(-se) pudiese, pudieses, pudiese, pudiésemos, pudieseis, pudiesen
Present Participle	pudiendo

poner — **to put, place**

Present Indicative	pongo, pones, pone, ponemos, ponéis, ponen
Preterite	puse, pusiste, puso, pusimos, pusisteis, pusieron
Future	pondré, pondrás, pondrá, pondremos, pondréis, pondrán
Conditional	pondría, pondrías, pondría, pondríamos, pondríais, pondrían
Imperfect Subjunctive	(-ra) pusiera, pusieras, pusiera, pusiéramos, pusierais, pusieran
	(-se) pusiese, pusieses, pusiese, pusiésemos, pusieseis, puiesen

| Past Participle | puesto |
| Imperative | pon, poned |

querer	**to wish, want, love**
Present Indicative	quiero, quieres, quiere, queremos, queréis, quieren
Preterite	quise, quisiste, quiso, quisimos, quisisteis, quisieron
Future	querré, querrás, querrá, querremos, querréis, querrán
Conditional	querría, querrías, querría, querríamos, querríais, querrían
Present Subjunctive	quiera, quieras, quiera, queramos, queráis, quieran
Imperfect Subjunctive	(-ra) quisiera, quisieras, quisiera, quisiéramos, quisierais, quisieran
	(-se) quisiese, quisieses, quisiese, quisiésemos, quisieseis, quisiesen

saber	**to know**
Present Indicative	sé, sabes, sabe, sabemos, sabéis, saben
Preterite	supe, supiste, supo, supimos, supisteis, supieron
Future	sabré, sabrás, sabrá, sabremos, sabréis, sabrán
Conditional	sabría, sabrías, sabría, sabríamos, sabríais, sabrían
Present Subjunctive	sepa, sepas, sepa, sepamos, sepáis, sepan
Imperfect Subjunctive	(-ra) supiera, supieras, supiera, supiéramos, supierais, supieran
	(-se) supiese, supieses, supiese, supiésemos, supieseis, supiesen

salir	**to go out, leave**
Present Indicative	salgo, sales, sale, salimos, salís, salen
Future	saldré, saldrás, saldrá, saldremos, saldréis, saldrán
Conditional	saldría, saldrías, saldría, saldríamos, saldríais, saldrían

| Present Subjunctive | salga, salgas, salga, salgamos, salgáis, salgan |
| Imperative | sal, salid |

ser   **to be**

Present Indicative	soy, eres, es, somos, sois, son
Imperfect Indicative	era, eras, era, éramos, erais, eran
Preterite	fui, fuiste, fue, fuimos, fuisteis, fueron
Present Subjunctive	sea, seas, sea, seamos, seáis, sean
Imperfect Subjunctive	(-ra) fuera, fueras, fuera, fuéramos, fuerais, fueran
	(se) fuese, fueses, fuese, fuésemos, fueseis, fuesen
Imperative	sé, sed

tener   **to have**

Present Indicative	tengo, tienes, tiene, tenemos, tenéis, tienen
Preterite	tuve, tuviste, tuvo, tuvimos, tuvisteis, tuvieron
Future	tendré, tendrás, tendrá, tendremos, tendréis, tendrán
Conditional	tendría, tendrías, tendría, tendríamos, tendríais, tendrían
Present Subjunctive	tenga, tengas, tenga, tengamos, tengáis, tengan
Imperfect Subjunctive	(-ra) tuviera, tuvieras, tuviera, tuviéramos, tuvierais, tuvieran
	(-se) tuviese, tuvieses, tuviese, tuviésemos, tuvieseis, tuviesen
Imperative	ten, tened

traer   **to bring**

Present Indicative	traigo, traes, trae, traemos, traéis, traen
Preterite	traje, trajiste, trajo, trajimos, trajisteis, trajeron
Present Subjunctive	traiga, traigas, traiga, traigamos, traigáis, traigan
Imperfect Subjunctive	(-ra) trajera, trajeras, trajera, trajéramos, trajerais, trajeran
	(-se) trajese, trajeses, trajese, trajésemos, trajeseis, trajesen

Present Participle   trayendo
Past Participle   traído

valer   **to be worth**
Present Indicative   valgo, vales, vale, valemos, valéis, valen
Future   valdré, valdrás, valdrá, valdremos, valdréis, valdrán
Conditional   valdría, valdrías, valdría, valdríamos, valdríais, valdrían
Present Subjunctive   valga, valgas, valga, valgamos, valgáis, valgan
Imperative   val(e), valed

venir   **to come**
Present Indicative   vengo, vienes, viene, venimos, venís, vienen
Preterite   vine, viniste, vino, vinimos, vinisteis, vinieron
Future   vendré, vendrás, vendrá, vendremos, vendréis, vendrán
Conditional   vendría, vendrías, vendría, vendríamos, vendríais, vendrían
Present Subjunctive   venga, vengas, venga, vengamos, vengáis, vengan
Imperfect Subjunctive   (-ra) viniera, vinieras, viniera, viniéramos, vinierais, vinieran
(-se) viniese, vinieses, viniese, viniésemos, vinieseis, viniesen
Present Participle   viniendo
Imperative   ven, venid

ver   **to see**
Present Indicative   veo, ves, ve, vemos, veis, ven
Imperfect Indicative   veía, veías, veía, veíamos, veíais, veían
Present Subjunctive   vea, veas, vea, veamos, veáis, vean
Past Participle   visto

SENTENCE STRUCTURE

9 Sentence Structure and Word Order

HOW TO STRUCTURE A SENTENCE

The structure and word order of Spanish sentences often does not correspond to English usage. (For word order of specific parts of speech—adjectives, adverbs, pronouns, etc.—see section on the appropriate part of speech.) *Frequently, word order in Spanish is variable,* and considerably more flexible than in English. In the following simple sentence with a linking verb, four different word orders may be used.

	Subject	Verb	Adj. Complement
English:	The landscape is impressive.		

	Subject	Verb	Adj. Complement
Spanish:	**El paisaje es impresionante.**		

Verb	Adjective	Subject
Es impresionante el paisaje.		

Verb	Subject	Adjective
Es el paisaje impresionante.		

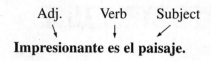

Adj.　　　Verb　　Subject

Impresionante es el paisaje.

RULE

In sentences with more syntactical elements, several word orders are also permissible in many instances (particularly to shift the emphasis from one element to another).

　　　　　　　　Subj.　Verb.　D. Obj.　Prep. Phrase

English:　　　Paul bought a ring for his fiancée.

Spanish:　　　**Pablo compró un anillo para su novia.**

　　　　　　　　　　　or

Compró Pablo un anillo para su novia.
Pablo compró para su novia un anillo.
Para su novia compró Pablo un anillo.

PITFALL

Other word arrangement of this same sentence would be possible in Spanish. At times in literature a seemingly illogical order has been employed by an author for poetic or dramatic effect, or for the sake of meter or rhyme.

> . . . **la política he estudiado**
> **de los brutos enseñado,**
> **advertido de las aves,**
> **y de los astros suaves**
> **los círculos he medido.**
> (Calderón, *La vida es sueño*)

As a step toward a clearer translation into English, the lines of Calderón might be rearranged in a more direct manner:

> . . . **he estudiado la política, enseñado de los brutos, advertido de las aves, y he medido los círculos de los astros suaves.**

PITFALL

Whereas in English the most common word order in a declarative sentence is **subject + verb + object** (or adverb or phrase), in Spanish the order is frequently **object (or other element) + verb + subject**. With experience in reading and speaking Spanish, one comes to accept the Spanish order as normal (*i.e.* verb preceding the subject).

English: It's true but my father doesn't believe it.

Spanish: **Es verdad pero no lo cree mi padre.**

English: They saw Julius in Paris.

Spanish: **A Julio le vieron en París.**

A noun direct object cannot precede a subject if there is the possibility of confusion between the two. In Spanish the preposition *a* is sometimes used before the direct object to distinguish it from the subject.

> **La leyenda vence a la historia.**
> Legend conquers history.

VERBS

PITFALL

Spanish does not permit the use of the verb "to do" as an auxiliary or helping verb. Where some form of "do" is used in English in phrasing a question, the Spanish translation will have only a single form of the verb.

English: *Do you want* to leave now?
Spanish: *¿Quieres* **salir ahora?**

English: *Did* Louis *receive* the letter I wrote to him?
Spanish: *¿Recibió* **Luis la carta que le escribí?**

English: *Does* the president *speak* French?
Spanish: *¿Habla* **francés el presidente?**

PITFALL

Unlike English, Spanish does not allow any word to come between the auxiliary verb *haber* and the past participle of the main verb in the compound tense.

English: They *have* already *arrived.*
Spanish: **Ya** *han llegado.*

English: She told me that they *had* not *called* us.
Spanish: **Me dijo que no nos** *habían llamado.*

THE USE OF *NO*

———————————————— RULE ————————————————

A common error in word order—resulting from literal, word-for-word translation—is the placement of the Spanish negative *no* in the exact position as its English equivalent not. *No* must always precede the verb in Spanish, and the only elements that may stand between it and the verb are pronoun objects (direct, indirect, reflexive).

English: That is *not* important.
INCORRECT SPANISH: **Eso es no importante.**
CORRECT SPANISH: *Eso no es importante.*

English: They have *not* spoken to her yet.
INCORRECT SPANISH: **Ellos le han no hablado todavía.**
CORRECT SPANISH: *Ellos no le han hablado todavía.*

194

SENTENCE MEANINGS AND WORD PLACEMENT

PITFALL

A different word order in a sentence can change its meaning entirely. In the following examples, the placement of *algo* and *un ensayo* determine the meaning of the sentences in which they are used.

> **Tengo algo que hacer.**
> I have something to do. (something I plan to do)
>
> **Tengo que hacer algo.**
> I have to do something. (something I am obligated to do)
>
> **Pablo tiene un ensayo que escribir.**
> Paul has an essay to write.
>
> **Pablo tiene que escribir un ensayo.**
> Paul has to write an essay.

PARALLEL CONSTRUCTION

PITFALL

Care should be paid to proper usage when writing parallel constructions both in Spanish and in English.

English: They must listen to me and help my friends.
INCORRECT SPANISH: **Deben escucharme y ayudan a mis amigos.**
CORRECT SPANISH: *Deben escucharme y ayudar a mis amigos.*

(The incorrect translation of the English "help" results from misreading the English sentence. Both "listen to" and "help" are infinitives dependent on the main verb "must." *Ayudan* would mean "they help.")

10 Punctuation and Division Into Syllables

PUNCTUATION
COMMON MARKS OF PUNCTUATION

English	Sign	Spanish
apostrophe	'	apóstrofo
asterisk	*	asterisco
braces	{ }	corchetes
brackets	[ ]	paréntesis cuadrados (angulares)
colon	:	dos puntos
comma	,	coma
dash	—	raya
diaeresis	..	diéresis (or crema)
exclamation point	¡ and !	principio de exclamación (¡) and fin de exclamación (!)
hyphen	-	guión
parentheses	( )	paréntesis
period	.	punto
question mark	¿ and ?	principio de interrogación fin de interrogación
quotation marks	" "	comillas
semicolon	;	punto y coma
suspension points	. . .	puntos suspensivos

Question Marks—and Interrogative Words

──────────────────── RULE ────────────────────

For questions, an inverted question mark is placed at the beginning of the sentence in addition to the final question mark.

────────────────────────────────────

¿Viene Juan?

Note that an accent mark is always necessary on all interrogative words (e.g. *¿quién?*, *¿qué?*, *¿como?*, and others.) The accent is also required in indirect or implied questions within a sentence.

> **Yo no sé *quién* es ella.**
> I don't know who she is.

> **Me pregunto *qué* buscas.**
> I wonder what you're looking for.

PITFALL

Since the inverted question mark must be placed where the question begins, it is not necessarily used at the beginning of a sentence.

> **Si lo hubieras sabido, ¿habrías firmado el documento?**
> If you had known, would you have signed the document?

(In this example the independent clause contains the question.)

The Exclamation Point

──────────────────── RULE ────────────────────

The inverted exclamation point must always begin an exclamatory sentence.

> **¡Qué lastima!**   What a shame!

The Dash

———————————— RULE ————————————

In Spanish the dash is used in dialogue to denote change of speaker.

—Pero piensa Ud. pasar la noche aquí?
—Sí; ¿por qué no?
—Hará frío.
—Eso no importa.

The Diaeresis

PITFALL

The diaeresis, which is used rarely in Spanish, is placed over the letter *u* in combinations of *gue* and *gui* when either has the **gw** sound.

lingüística   (linguistic)
averigüe   (pres. subj. of *averiguar*)
vergüenza   (shame)

This mark (¨) is called a "*crema*" in Spanish.

NUMBERS AND PUNCTUATION

———————————— RULE ————————————

Punctuation for numbers is the exact opposite of English in some Spanish-speaking countries. A decimal point is used in place of a comma, e.g. 15,000 is expressed as 15.000 in Spanish. The comma is used in place of the decimal point; thus 1.5 in English becomes 1,5 in Spanish.

PITFALL

The period is not written in numbers indicating years: 1971, 1492, 2000.

———————————— RULE ————————————

The conjunction *o* is accented when between numbers to avoid confusion with (5 ó 6, 10 ó más).

CAPITALIZATION

———————————— RULE ————————————

The capitalization of Spanish words is not as extensive as in English. **Nouns and adjectives denoting nationality, religion, affiliation, names of languages, names of the months of the year, and names of the days of the week are generally *not* capitalized.** (On the other hand, names of countries and continents do begin with a capital letter.)

un inglés	an Englishman
un católico	a Catholic
un judío	a Jew
el rey español	the Spanish king
francés	French
domingo	Sunday
diciembre	December

But:

Europa	Europe
el Canadá	Canada
Rusia	Russia

———————————— RULE ————————————

Titles are not capitalized in Spanish except when abbreviated.

el señor Ortiz	Mister Ortiz
el general Powell	General Powell
doña Inés	doña is not translated into English

But:

el Sr. Ortiz	Mr. Ortiz
el Gral. Patton	Gen. Patton
Dª Inés	

PITFALL

Usually accent marks are not carried over capital letters—although they are permissible.

> **Este** or **Éste**
> **Oigame usted** or **Óigame usted**

PITFALL

In the titles of books, plays, motion pictures, etc., only the first word of the title and names of persons and countries within the title are normally capitalized. (Sometimes words that are given a symbolical or thematic importance within the work are also capitalized.)

> *La guerra del fin del mundo*   (Vargas Llosa)
> (*The War of the End of the World*)

> *La rebelión de las masas*   (Ortega y Gasset)
> (*The Revolt of the Masses*)

> *Lo que el viento se llevó*   (Mitchell)
> (*Gone With the Wind*)

> *El Cristo de Velázquez*   (Unamuno)
> (*The Christ of Velazquez*)

DIVISION INTO SYLLABLES

PITFALL

A **single consonant** (including the combinations *ch*, *ll*, and *rr*) goes with the following vowel.

> **to/ma   ni/ño   le/che   ca/lla/do   ye/rro**

PITFALL

Two consonants are separated, except if the second is *l* or *r*.

pal/ma	**car/ta**	**in/fier/no**	
	But		
pue/blo	**o/tro**	**a/pren/der**	**te/a/tro**

PITFALL

In groups of **three consonants** only the last goes with the following vowel, except if there is an inseparable combination involving *l* or *r*.

ins/tan/te   **trans/fe/rir**   **cons/cien/cia**

PITFALL

Any combination of **two vowels involving *u* or *i*** and pronounced together, form one syllable—a *diphthong*.

vein/te   **rui/do**   **sois**   **ai/re**   **Ma/rio**

PITFALL

A **written accent on *i* or *u*** breaks the diphthong and creates two separate syllables.

Ma/rí/a	**can/ta/rí/a**	
li/bre/rí/a	**le/í/do**	**rí/o**

PITFALL

All other vowels placed together are separated. (Two strong vowels—*a*, *e*, *o*,—can never form a single syllable.)

ca/os	**re/al**	**le/er**
cre/e/ré	**te/a/tro**	**to/a/lla**

SPECIAL TOPICS
11 Measurements

NUMBERS

There are three types of numbers in Spanish. They are **cardinal**, **ordinal**, and **collective**.

CARDINAL NUMBERS

Cardinal Numbers in Spanish

uno, una	**1**
dos	**2**
tres	**3**
cuatro	**4**
cinco	**5**
seis	**6**
siete	**7**
ocho	**8**
nueve	**9**
diez	**10**
once	**11**
doce	**12**
trece	**13**
catorce	**14**
quince	**15**
diez y seis or dieciséis	**16**
diez y siete or diecisiete	**17**
diez y ocho or dieciocho	**18**
diez y nueve or diecinueve	**19**

veinte	**20**
veinte y uno or veintiuno	**21**
veinte y dos or veintidós	**22**
treinta	**30**
treinta y uno	**31**
cuarenta	**40**
cuarenta y uno	**41**
cincuenta	**50**
sesenta	**60**
setenta	**70**
ochenta	**80**
noventa	**90**
ciento (cien)	**100**
ciento uno	**101**
doscientos (as)	**200**
trescientos (as)	**300**
cuatrocientos (as)	**400**
quinientos (as)	**500**
seiscientos (as)	**600**
setecientos (as)	**700**
ochocientos (as)	**800**
novecientos (as)	**900**
mil	**1,000**
dos mil	**2,000**
doscientos (as) mil	**200,000**
un millón	**1,000,000**
dos millones	**2,000,000**

The Use of *y*

——————————————— RULE ———————————————

The conjunction **y** is used to form all compound numbers from 31 through 99.

————————————————————————————————

treinta y cinco	thirty-five
noventa y siete	ninety-seven

PITFALL

The numbers 16 through 19 and 21 through 29 have two forms in Spanish, but they are more frequently written as one word.

> **diecinueve** (or **diez y nueve**)—nineteen
> **veintitrés** (or **veinte y tres**)—twenty-three

PITFALL

In English we may say "two hundred seventeen" or "two hundred *and* seventeen." However, in Spanish *y* is not used between hundreds, thousands, or millions and the next numeral in the series.

> **doscientos diecisiete kilómetros**—217 kilometers.
> **dos mil trece metros**—2013 meters

Uno, Ciento, Mil, Millón

—————————————— RULE ——————————————

Uno alone or in compound numbers drops the *o* before a masculine noun. When the number *uno* immediately precedes a plural noun, *un* or *una* is used, depending on the gender of the noun.

veintiún años	twenty-one years
But	
Sólo me dio uno.	He only gave me one.
treinta y una libras	thirty-one pounds
sesenta y un años de edad	sixty-one years old

PITFALL

Cardinal numbers are invariable with the exception of **uno** and the multiple numbers of **ciento** (*doscientos, trescientos,* etc.). These must all agree in gender with the noun they modify.

página veintiuna	page twenty-one
doscientas personas	two hundred persons
quinientos obreros	five hundred workers

PITFALL

Uno is omitted before **cien** (*to*) and *mil* unless the number is ambiguous.

cien soldados	a (one) hundred soldiers
ciento diez	one hundred ten
mil personas	a thousand people
cien mil pesos	a hundred thousand pesos

But

doscientos un mil	201,000

PITFALL

Ciento becomes **cien** before nouns and before a number it multiplies. (Also see section on Adjectives.)

cien hombres	a hundred men
cien mujeres	a hundred women
cien mil dólares	a hundred thousand dollars
cien millones de pesetas	a hundred million pesetas

PITFALL

Special attention should be given to the Spanish numbers 500, 700, and 900 because of the change in the spelling of **cinco, siete,** and **nueve** in their formation.

five hundred = *quinientos* (not **cincocientos**)
seven hundred = *setecientos* (not **sietecientos**)
nine hundred = *novecientos* (not **nuevecientos**)

PITFALL

Spanish does not count by hundreds above 900. In English we frequently say nineteen hundred (1900) instead of "one thousand nine hundred." In Spanish the number 1900 can only be expressed as *mil novecientos* (NEVER *diecinueve cientos*).

1492	**mil cuatrocientos noventa y dos**
1987	**mil novecientos ochenta y siete**

PITFALL

Since the number *millón* is a noun, it must be preceded by the indefinite article *un*. The preposition *de* is required with a following noun.

Gironella escribió la novela *Un millón de muertos*.
Gironella wrote the novel *Un millón de muertos*.

Madrid tiene más de cuatro millones de habitantes.
Madrid has more than four million inhabitants.

ORDINAL NUMBERS

Ordinal Numbers in Spanish

primero	first
segundo	second
tercero	third
cuarto	fourth
quinto	fifth
sexto	sixth
séptimo	seventh
octavo	eighth
noveno or **nono**	ninth
décimo	tenth
undécimo	eleventh
duodécimo	twelfth

decimotercio or **decimotercero**	thirteenth
decimocuarto	fourteenth
decimoquinto	fifteenth
decimosexto	sixteenth
decimoséptimo	seventeenth
decimoctavo	eighteenth
decimonoveno or **decimonono**	nineteenth
vigésimo	twentieth
vigésimo prim(er)o	twenty-first
vigésimo segundo	twenty-second
trigésimo	thirtieth
cuadragésimo	fortieth
quincuagésimo	fiftieth
sexagésimo	sixtieth
septuagésimo	seventieth
octogésimo	eightieth
nonagésimo	ninetieth
centésimo	hundredth
centésimo prim(er)o	hundred and first
centésimo segundo	hundred and second
ducentésimo	two hundredth
tricentésimo	three hundredth
cuadringentésimo	four hundredth
quingentésimo	five hundredth
sexcentésimo	six hundredth
septingentésimo	seven hundredth
octingentésimo	eight hundredth
noningentésimo	nine hundredth
milésimo	thousandth
dos milésimo	two thousandth
doscientos milésimo	two hundred thousandth
millonésimo	millionth
dos millonésimo	two millionth

Note: In most cases the simpler cardinal numbers may be used in place of the ordinals above *décimo* [10th].

———————————————— RULE ————————————————

The ordinals *primero* and *tercero* drop the final *o* before a masculine singular noun. (Also see section on Adjectives.)

    el primer presidente   the first president
    el tercer ejemplar   the third copy

PITFALL

Ordinal numbers are abbreviated by adding the final syllable, or the final letter, of the number to the Arabic numeral. The ending must agree in gender with the noun it modifies.

    el 1ro **de enero**
           or   the first of January
    el 1° **de enero**

    la 2da **lección**
           or   the second lesson
    la 2^{a} **lección**

Position

PITFALL

Ordinal numbers may be placed before or after the noun. (Also see section on Adjectives.)

    el primer día   the first day
        or
    el día primero

PITFALL

Cardinal numbers used in place of ordinals generally follow the noun.

    el siglo XX (el siglo veinte)
    the twentieth century

el día 17 (el día diecisiete)
the seventeenth day

PITFALL

In addresses where a floor number is given the Arabic numeral is generally followed by *o*.

Juan Alvarez, 33	(The street address is "No. 33 Juan
4° A	Alvarez" and the apartment is
13080 Castellón	"Apt. A" on the fourth floor)
España	

Royalty

PITFALL

With names of royalty and popes, ordinal numbers are used in Spanish only through *décimo* (10th). For translating English ordinals into Spanish above *tenth*, the cardinal numbers are used. Note that the definite article is omitted between the given name of the person and the number, and that *nono* replaces *noveno* in titles.

Carlos V (Carlos Quinto)
Charles the Fifth

Alfonso XIII (Alfonso Trece)
Alfonso the Thirteenth

Papa Juan XXIII (Papa Juan veintitrés)
Pope John the Twenty-third

Pío IX (Pío Nono)
Pius the Ninth

Collective Numbers

Collective Numbers in Spanish

un par	a pair

una docena	a dozen
una gruesa	a gross (144)
una quincena	a fortnight (15 days)
una veintena	a score
un centenar	hundred
un millar	thousand
un millón	million

---------------------------- RULE ----------------------------

The collective nouns are followed by *de* when used with a noun.

un par de zapatos	a pair of shoes
una docena de huevos	a dozen eggs

PITFALL

The collective noun *un par* is not used with *pantalones* (pants, trousers) in Spanish.

English: I'm going to buy a pair of trousers.

Spanish: **Voy a comprar pantalones** (or **un pantalón**).

Fractions

---------------------------- RULE ----------------------------

In Spanish the cardinal numbers are used for the numerator of a fraction as in English.

2/3	=	*dos* **tercios**
3/4	=	*tres* **cuartos**

---------------------------- RULE ----------------------------

From 1/4 through 10/10 the ordinal numbers are used for the denominator. "Half" is translated by *medio* and "third" by *tercio*.

2/4	=	**dos** *cuartos*
5/7	=	**cinco** *séptimos*

9/10	=	nueve *décimos*
1/2	=	un *medio*
1/3	=	un *tercio*

—————————————— RULE ——————————————

For fractions from 1/11, the denominator is formed by adding *-avo* to the cardinal numbers. Except for *siete* and *nueve* the final vowel of the cardinal number is dropped before adding the ending. In the fractions 11th through 15th, the *c* in the cardinal number changes to *z* before *-avo*.

1/11	=	un onzavo
1/12	=	un dozavo
1/13	=	un trezavo
1/14	=	un catorzavo
1/15	=	un quinzavo
1/16	=	un dieciseisavo
1/17	=	un diecisieteavo
1/19	=	sun diecinueveavo
1/20	=	un veintavo
1/30	=	un treintavo
1/40	=	un cuarentavo
1/100	=	un centavo (not cientavo)

PITFALL

Fractions may also be expressed by using *parte*.

> la cuarta parte = 1/4 (un cuarto)
> (las) dos terceras partes 2/3 (dos tercios)

Medio and *Mitad* for "Half"

—————————————— RULE ——————————————

Medio as an adjective means "half." It agrees with the noun it modifies and may occur in Spanish where a noun is preferred in English.

Compró *media* docena de rosas.
He bought half a dozen roses or "a half dozen roses."

PITFALL

Medio is sometimes used as an adverb, and its form is then invariable.

Estábamos *medio* asustados y *medio* sorprendidos.
We were half scared and half surprised.

PITFALL

Medio normally precedes the noun it modifies, but in isolated cases it may follow.

media hora	half (an) hour

But

dos horas y media	two and a half hours

("hora" is understood with *media*)

--- RULE ---

Mitad is the Spanish noun that means "half."

Vendió la mitad de sus bienes.
He sold half of his possessions.

Tenemos la mitad más una de las acciones.
We have 51% ("a half plus one") of the stock (shares).

TIME EXPRESSIONS
TELLING TIME

--- RULE ---

When telling clock time, the verb *ser* is used. A singular form of the verb is used with *una* (hora) (one o'clock). With the hours *dos* (two) through *doce* (twelve) a plural verb is required.

Es la una y media	It's one-thirty.
Será la una.	It's probably one o'clock.

But

Son las tres y cuarto	It's three-fifteen.
Eran las cinco.	It was five o'clock
Serán las nueve menos cuarto.	It's probably a quarter until nine.

PITFALL

Minutes after a certain hour are added to the hour and are connected by *y* if the time is not past the half hour (2:05 = *las dos y cinco*). After the half hour, the minutes are usually subtracted from the following hour (that is *las tres menos cinco* ["three minus five"] = 2:55 or "five minutes until three"). However, in everyday usage one might hear 2:55 expressed as *las dos cincuenta y cinco*. *Cuarto* or *quince* may be used for quarter hours, and *media* or *treinta* express the half hour.

Son las siete y cuarto	It's seven-fifteen.
or	
Son las siete y quince.	
Son las diez y media.	It's ten-thirty.
or	
Son las diez y treinta	
Eran las diez menos cuarto.	It was a quarter to ten (or 9:45).

PITFALL

In airline, train, and bus schedules a 24 hour clock is customarily used. Counting begins at one minute past midnight; 1 PM becomes 13.00 *(trece horas)*, 2 PM becomes 14.00 *(catorce horas)*, and 12 midnight is 24.00 *(veinticuatro horas)*.

El Talgo llega a las quince (y) veinte.
The Talgo (rapid Spanish train) arrives at 3:20 PM (or "15:20").

Tomamos el Vuelo 557 a las 19.05.
We're taking Flight 557 at 7:05 PM.

However, in such schedules, minutes cannot be subtracted from the following hour as in conversation.

El vuelo 910 de Buenos Aires llegará a las 9.40.
Flight 910 from Buenos Aires will arrive at 9:40 AM.

PITFALL

Another way to express time **before the hour,** in addition to *menos,* is with the verb *faltar* (to be missing or lacking).

Faltan diez minutos para las seis.
It's ten minutes to six. (Literally: Ten minutes are lacking for six.)

PITFALL

The Spanish equivalent to "a little past the hour" is the word *pico.*

Llegaremos a casa a las siete y pico.
We'll arrive home a little after seven.

PITFALL

To express **approximate time** ("around" or "about") in Spanish, *a eso de* (about), *a fines de* (around the end of), *a mediados de* (around [in] the middle of), and *a principios de* (around the beginning of) are frequently used.

a eso de las once	about 11 o'clock
a fines del mes (año)	around the end of the month (year)
a mediados de octubre	in the middle of October
a principios del mes	around the beginning of the month.

Tiempo versus *Vez* for the English "Time"

--- RULE ---

The word *tiempo* translates the English "time" when it refers to scientific measurement or to the word in a philosophic or abstract sense. *Tiempo* also has the meaning of "weather" in certain expressions.

Amigo mío, aquí no existe el Tiempo.
My friend, Time doesn't exist here.

El tiempo no importa a los viajeros que tienen dinero.
Time doesn't matter to travellers who have money.

Esta tarde hace muy buen tiempo.
This afternoon the weather is very nice.

PITFALL

Although *tiempo* refers to the total idea of measured time, the word cannot be used when asking a specific time of day. In such a question *hora* is correct.

English: What time is it?
INCORRECT SPANISH: **¿Qué tiempo es?**
CORRECT SPANISH: *¿Qué hora es?*

PITFALL

Tiempo may never be used in the sense of "occasion" or "diversion." To express the idea of having a good time, the expressions *pasarlo bien* or *divertirse* are appropriate (never *tener un buen tiempo!*).

English: This summer I'm going to have a great time.
INCORRECT SPANISH: **Este verano voy a tener un muy buen tiempo.**
CORRECT SPANISH: *Este verano voy a pasarlo (muy) bien.*
                                      or
                         Este verano voy a divertirme mucho.

RULE

To express the idea of "occasion" or when referring to a repeated occurrence or a number of times in a series, *vez* translates the English word "time."

English:	This time there's no problem.
INCORRECT SPANISH:	**Este tiempo no hay problema.**
CORRECT SPANISH:	***Esta vez no hay problema.***

Common Expressions with *vez*

---

a la vez (also: **al mismo tiempo**)	at the same time
a veces	sometimes
algunas veces	sometimes
cada vez	each time
dos veces	twice (two times)
en vez de	instead of
otra vez	again (another time)
una vez	once
tal vez	perhaps
las más veces	most of the time
muchas veces	often (many times)
raras veces	rarely
repetidas veces	over and over again
varias veces	several times

Duration of Time

In English, time expressions involving an action that begins in the past and continues into the present are normally expressed by the *present perfect progressive* form of the verb ("I *have been writing* for several hours"), and those involving actions beginning in the past and lasting for a period in the past (but now completed) are expressed by the *past perfect progressive* ("I *had been writing* for several hours"). Spanish employs three quite different constructions. They can best be understood by comparing the formula for the English construction with the equivalent Spanish formulas.

Grammatical Structure

English Formula:	Pres. Perf. Progressive of verb + for + time.
Spanish Formulas:	**Hace** + time + **que** + present tense of verb.
or	Present tense of verb + **desde** + **hace** + time
or	**Lleva** + time + present participle.
English:	She has been waiting for an hour.
Spanish:	**Hace una hora que espera.**

or

Espera desde hace una hora.

or

Lleva una hora esperando.

PITFALL

If the action began in the past and ended in the past, the English verb becomes past perfect progressive; in Spanish the present tense verbs shift to the imperfect.

She had been waiting for an hour.
Hacía una hora que esperaba.

or

Esperaba desde hacía una hora.

or

Llevaba una hora esperando.

RULE

To express the fact that someone has not been doing something for a certain length of time, *sin* + infinitive may be used.

Lleva una hora sin hablar.
He hasn't said anything for an hour.

or

He hasn't been saying anything for an hour.

RULE

The English "ago" preceded by a time expression is expressed in Spanish by *hace* + a time expression.

El presidente Lincoln murió hace más de cien años.
or: **Hace más**
de cien años que murió el presidente Lincoln.
President Lincoln died more than a hundred years ago.
(Literally: "It makes more than a hundred years that President Lincoln died.")

MISCELLANEOUS EXPRESSIONS OF TIME
Past, Present, and Future

Past Time

anoche	last night
anteanoche	the night before last
ayer	yesterday
anteayer	the day before yesterday
ayer por la mañana	yesterday morning
(tarde, noche)	(afternoon, evening)
en el mes	in the month just past
próximo pasado	

Present Time

hoy	today
hoy día	nowadays
ahora	now
en este momento	at this moment

Future Time

mañana	tomorrow
mañana por	tomorrow morning
la mañana	

218

(tarde, noche)	(afternoon, evening)
pasado mañana	the day after tomorrow
mañana y pasado	tomorrow and the next day
de ayer en ocho días	a week from yesterday
del (viernes) en ocho días	a week from (Friday)

Time and Day Divisions

Divisions of Time

año bisiesto	leap year
días laborables	weekdays (workdays)
días de trabajo	weekdays (workdays)
todos los días	every day
un día sí y otro no	every other day
fin de semana	week end
quince días	two weeks (fortnight)
una década	a decade
un siglo	a century

Divisions of the Day

madrugada	early morning (from midnight to sunrise)
mañana	morning (sunrise to noon)
tarde	afternoon (noon to sunset)
noche	evening, night (sunset to midnight)

Note that *noche* can popularly mean the hours from sunset to sunrise.

> **No llegaron hasta las dos de la madrugada.**
>   or
> **No llegaron hasta las dos de la noche.**
> They did not arrive until 2:00 a.m.

Common Time Expressions

a la madrugada	at an early hour
al amanecer	at dawn (daybreak)
al anochecer	at dusk (nightfall)
al día siguiente	on the next day, on the following day
de día	by day, in the daytime
de noche	by night, at night, in the night
medianoche	midnight
mediodía	noon
por la mañana	early in the morning
temprano	
(tarde, noche)	(afternoon, evening)

Writing Dates

———————————————— RULE ————————————————

When writing dates in Spanish, numbers must precede months.

English:	August 31, 1997
Spanish:	**el 31 de agosto de 1997**

PITFALL

Although the artide *el* is used with the number of the day, in the heading of a letter it is frequently omitted.

15 de febrero de 1996

DISTANCES AND WEIGHT
OBJECT DIMENSIONS

Nouns and Adjectives Used for Object Dimensions

Noun	Adjective
la altura (height)	**alto** (tall, high)
la anchura (width)	**ancho** (wide)

el espesor (thickness)	**grueso** (thick)
la longitud (length)	**largo** (long)
la profundidad (depth)	**profundo** (deep)

—————————————— RULE ——————————————

Dimension may be expressed with *tener* or with *ser*.

El aeropuerto tiene una altura de 246 metros sobre el nivel del mar.
The airport is (at an altitude of) 246 meters above sea level.

Este coche tiene catorce pies de largo.
This car is fourteen feet long. (Note that when the dimension follows the number, the adjective form is used rather than the noun.)

La profundidad del lago es de veinte metros.
The depth of the lake is twenty meters.

PITFALL

In asking what the dimension of an object is, the interrogative pronoun *¿cuánto . . .?* is used. It is followed by *de* + **an adjective**.

¿Cuánto de ancho tiene el cuarto?
How wide is the room?

¿Cuánto de largo es el río Orinoco?
How long is the Orinoco River?

METRIC SYSTEM *(SISTEMA MÉTRICO)*

PITFALL

Spanish-speaking countries use the metric system for measurements rather than the inches, feet, miles, pounds, etc. used in the United States (and few other places). For example, the distance between points is measured in kilometers (*kilómetros*), not miles. Since a kilometer is only 5/8 of a mile, distances posted on signs or encountered in books and newspapers seem greater to the English-speaker than they actually are. (For example, 968 *kilómetros* = 605 miles.) However, common U.S. measurements may be expressed in Spanish even though they are not normally used.

pulgada (inch)   **milla** (mile)
pie (foot)   **libra** (pound)

Weights and Measures (Pesos y Medidas)

Linear Measures (*Medidas de longitud*)

1 centímetro = 10 milímetros	0.3937 inches
1 metro = 100 centímetros	39.37 inches or
	1.094 yards
1 kilómetro = 1000 metros	0.6214 mile

Square Measures (*Medidas cuadradas*)

1 centímetro cuadrado	0.155 square inch
1 metro cuadrado	10.764 feet
1 kilómetro cuadrado	247.1 acres or
	0.3861 square mile
1 hectárea	2.47 acres

Measure of Capacity (*Medida de capacidad*)

1 litro = 1000 centímetros cúbicos	1.057 quarts
	or .264 gallon

Weights (*Pesos*)

1 gramo	.035 ounces
1 kilo	2.2046 pounds
1 quintal = 100 kilos	220.46 pounds
(in Castilla = **46 kilos**)	

MONETARY SYSTEMS

In the monetary systems of Spanish-speaking countries the decimal system is standard, and the basic unit *(peso, bolívar, etc.)* is divided into 100 parts. Coins or paper money exist in varying denominations depending on the value of the basic unit. Exchange rates vary considerably and are subject to considerable fluctuation in certain countries.

Principal Currencies in the Spanish-Speaking World

Argentina - Peso
Chile - Peso
Colombia - Peso
Ecuador - Sucre
Mexico - Peso

Peru - Sol (Nuevo Sol)
Spain - Peseta
Uruguay - Peso
(Nuevo peso)
Venezuela - Bolívar

12 Pronunciation, Accentuation, and Dialects

PRONUNCIATION

THE SPANISH ALPHABET

The Spanish alphabet has twenty-nine letters. (The Spanish Academy counts only twenty-eight.) *Ch*, *ll*, and *ñ* are considered separate single letters and have been treated as such in the alphabetization of Spanish words; however, the Association of Spanish Language Academies has now approved the inclusion of *ch* and *ll* under *c* and *l* in the future alphabetizing. Double *r* is alphabetized as in English. *W* is found only in foreign words, and retains its foreign pronunciation.

The Spanish Alphabet

Letter	Name	Approximate English Sound
a	a	Like *a* in English *father*, e.g *mano*, *coma*.
b	be	Like *b* in English *boat* when in the initial position or preceded by *m*. *bola*, *tumba*. In all other positions *b* is pronounced like *v* in English *over* except that the lips do not quite touch: *haber*, *tubo*.
c	ce	When followed by *e* or *i*, like *th* in English *thing* in Castilian, and like *c* in English *certain* in Latin American Spanish, e.g *cinco*, *amanecer*. When followed by *a*, *o* or *u* or a consonant, like *c* in English *can*, e.g. *callar*, *caja*, *pacto*.
ch	che	Like *ch* in English *such*, e.g. *leche*.
d	de	Pronounced like *d* in *dull*, e.g. *dar*, *vender* but like *th* in English *this* when between two vowels, and when final, e.g. *hado*, *usted*.

Letter	Name	Approximate English Sound
e	e	When followed by a single consonant or a vowel, or at the end of a word, pronounced like *a* in *gate*, e.g. *tema, café, verde*. When followed by more than one consonant or a single consonant at the end of a word, like the *e* in English *net*, e.g. *celda, ochenta, viven*.
f	efe	Like *f* in English *file*, e.g. *fama, efecto*.
g	ge	When followed by *e* or *i*, like *h* in English *hope*, e.g. *gitano, gesto*. When followed by *a, o,* or *u* or a consonant, pronounced like *g* in English *game*, e.g. *gallo, goma, gusto, gallego*.
h	hache	Always silent, e.g., *hambre, alcohol*.
i	i	Like *i* in English *machine*, e.g. *hilo, isla*. When preceded or followed by another vowel, it has the sound of the English *y*, e.g. *sierra, miedo*.
j	jota	Like *h* in English *hope*, e.g. *jugar, jaula*.
k	ka	Like English *k*, e.g *kilómetro*.
l	ele	Like *l* in English *large*, e.g. *le, largo, kilo*.
ll	elle	Like *lli* in *million* in Castilian, and like *y* in English *yet* in Latin American Spanish, e.g. *llorar, orilla*.
m	eme	Like *m* in English man, e.g. *mano, amigo*.
n	ene	Like *n* in English *now*, e.g. *nariz, poner* except before the hard *c* sound and *g*, when it is like *n* in English *think*, e.g. *rincón, ganga*.
ñ	eñe	Somewhat like *ny* in English *canyon*, e.g. *año, daño*.
o	o	Like the English *o* in *go*, however, pronounced with a short staccato sound, e.g. *como, orden, doctor*.
p	p	Like *p* in English *pan*, e.g. *palo, apoyo*.

Letter	Name	Approximate English Sound
q	cu	Like *c* in English *can*. It is always followed by *ue* or *ui* and the *u* is always silent, e.g *quejar*, *quitar*. The English *qu* is represented in Spanish by *cu*. e.g. *delincuente*.
r	ere	Trilled when in initial position and when preceded by *l*, *n*, or *s*, e.g. rato, alrededor, enrabiar, Israel. Otherwise pronounced with a slight trip of the tongue, e.g. *mero*, *loro*.
rr	erre	Trilled, e.g. *tierra*.
s	ese	In most cases like the *s* in English *sir*, e.g. *servir*, *masa*, *caso*. Before a voiced consonant (*b*, *d*, *hard g*, *l*, *m*, *n*,) like *z* in English *zoo* e.g. *esbelto*, *esdrújula*, *rasgo*, *eslovaco*, *esmero*, *mesnada*.
t	te	Like *t* in English *stand*, e.g. *tubo*, *quitar*.
u	u	Like *u* in English *rude*, e.g. *duque*, *pulir*. The *u* is silent in *gue*, *gui*, *que* and *qui*, e.g. *pague*, *guía*, *que*, *alguien*, but is pronounced in *güe* and *güi*, e.g. *averigüe*, *lingüística*. When followed by another vowel, it has the sound of English *w*, e.g. *juego*, *huevo*.
v	ve or uve	Like Spanish *b* in all of its positions, e.g. *vaca*, *uva*.
w	doble v (or doble u)	(Found only in foreign words.)
x	equis	Like *s* in English *sir* when followed by a consonant, e.g. *extranjero*. Between two vowels, *x* is pronounced like English *gs* e.g. *examen*, *exótico*.
y	ye or	The conjunction *y* is like the English *i* in *machine*.
	i griega	When next to or between two vowels, it is pronounced like the *y* in English *yet*, e.g. *yo*, *doy*, *soy*.
z	zeta	Like *th* in English *thing* in Castilian, and like *c* in English *certain* in Latin American Spanish, e.g. *zumo*, *zapato*, *izquierdo*.

Diphthongs

The weak vowels *i* (*y*) and *u* can combine with the strong vowels *a, e, o,* or with each other to form single syllables called diphthongs. In this case, the strong vowel keeps its full syllabic value while the weak vowel loses part of its value. However, these combinations are always pronounced as one syllable.

SPANISH DIPHTHONGS

Diphthong	Approximate English Sound	Example
ai/ay	like *i* in *time*	**baile, hay**
au	like *ow* in *now*	**jaula**
ei/ey	like *a* in *date*	**peine, rey**
eu	like *eh* + *oo*	**feudal**
oi/oy	like *oy* in *toy*	**boicot, doy**
ia	like *ya* in *yacht*	**estudiamos**
ie	like *ye* in *yet*	**miel**
io	like *yo* in *yoga*	**medio**
ua	like *wa* in *watt*	**cuatro**
ue	like *wa* in *wait*	**bueno**
ui	like *wee* in *week*	**cuidado**
uo	like *uo* in *quota*	**cuota**

Triphthongs

A triphthong is a combination of a stressed strong vowel between two weak vowels which forms a single syllable. Only four combinations exist in Spanish.

SPANISH TRIPHTHONGS

Triphthong	Approximate English Sound	Example
iai	like *yi* in *yipe*	**estudiáis**
iei	like English word *yea*	**estudiéis**
uai (uay)	like *wi* in *wine*	**continuáis, Paraguay**
uei (vey)	like *wa* in *wade*	**continuéis, buey**

Note: It should be kept in mind that the pronunciation aids supplied above are just that: aids. Language is not a series of isolated sounds. A person speaking Spanish will run many words together into natural groups, and the final sound of a word may be linked to the beginning sound of the following word. Fluency in the spoken language can only come from listening to and imitating whole sentences, and from expressing entire ideas—not isolated words.

ACCENTUATION
ENDINGS

——————————————— RULE ———————————————

Most words **ending in a consonant except *n* or *s***, are stressed on the last syllable.

juven*tud*, ver*mut*, ciu*dad*, profe*sor*

——————————————— RULE ———————————————

Most words that **end in a vowel or *n* or *s***, have the stress on the next to the last syllable.

*sa*ben, *cla*ses, *or*den, *po*zo

——————————————— RULE ———————————————

Words that are not pronounced according to these two rules must have an accent mark on the stressed syllable.

lec*ción*, *fá*cil, lucié*r*naga

PITFALL

Sometimes a singular accented word loses its accent when made plural.

lección	lecciones
festín	festines

The reverse is also true when a plural accented word is made singular.

jóvenes	joven
crímenes	crimen

In the examples given, a written accent was used to retain the pronunciation of the root word (*lección*, *festín*, *joven*, *crimen*) according to the rules for accentuation. The word *carácter* is an exception to the rule in that the stress shifts to another syllable in the plural and the written accent is no longer needed (*caracteres*).

Verbs Ending in -*iar*

PITFALL

Some verbs ending in -*iar* carry an accent mark on the *i* of the first, second, and third singular and the third person plural forms of both the present indicative and present subjunctive tenses. The accent does *not* occur in other tenses.

aliar(se)	(to ally, form an alliance)
ampliar	(to amplify, enlarge)
ataviar	(to dress, adorn)
calofriar(se)	(to become chilled)
contrariar	(to counteract, go against)
criar	(to raise, bring up)
chirriar	(to creak)
desataviar	(to put in disarray, undress)

desliar	(to untie)
enfriar	(to cool, chill)
escalofriar (se)	(to shiver)
espiar	(to spy on)
fiar, confiar	(to entrust, confide)
guiar	(to guide)
hastiar	(to bother, annoy)
liar	(to tie, bind)
piar	(to peep, chirp)
resfriar	(to cool, chill)
variar	(to vary, change)

Example of the above:

criar (to raise)	Present Indicative	Present Subjunctive
	crío	*críe*
	crías	*críes*
	cría	*críe*
	criamos	criemos
	criáis	criéis
	crían	*críen*

PITFALL

Other verbs follow the pattern of *estudiar* and do not carry the accent.

Estudiar (to study)	Present Indicative	Present Subjunctive
	estudio	**estudie**
	estudias	**estudies**
	estudia	**estudie**
	estudiamos	**estudiemos**
	estudiáis	**estudiéis**
	estudian	**estudien**

Verbs Ending in -*uar*

PITFALL

Verbs ending in -*uar* (except those ending in -*guar*) carry a written accent on the *u* of the first, second, and third singular and the third person plural forms of the present indicative and present subjunctive tenses. Example:

Continuar	Present Indicative	Present Subjunctive
(to continue)		
	continúo	*continúe*
	continúas	*continúe*
	continúa	*continúe*
	continuamos	**continuemos**
	continuáis	**continuéis**
	continúan	*continúen*

PRONOUNS
Object Pronouns

PITFALL

Often a written accent is required when object pronouns are added to present participles, infinitives or affirmative commands because the root word always retains its original stress.

Root word	With Object Pronouns
diga	**dígamelo**
comprar	**comprármelos**
pagando	**pagándosela**

If no accent were written on the correct syllable, the stress would be incorrectly shifted to another syllable, resulting in a violation of the rules of accentuation.

Demonstrative Pronouns

PITFALL

Demonstrative pronouns always have an accent while the demonstrative adjectives do not. The demonstrative pronoun is used nominally.

Demonstratives

Demonstrative Pronouns	Demonstrative Adjectives
éste, -a, -os, -as	**este, -a, -os, -as**
ése, -a, -os, -as	**ese, -a, -os, -as**
aquél, -lla, -llos, -llas	**aquel, -lla, -llos, -llas**

ADVERBS

PITFALL

Adverbs formed from adjectives with a written accent retain the accent even though the main stress falls on the adverbial ending *-mente*.

rápido	**rápidamente**
fácil	**fácilmente**

MISCELLANEOUS ACCENTUATION

PITFALL

Some Spanish words have the same spelling but one carries an accent to differentiate it from the other.

Accent/Meaning Variations

With Accent		Without Accent	
aún	(still, yet)	**aun**	(even)
dé	present subjunctive, **dar**	**de**	preposition

él	subject pronoun	**el**	definite article
más	adverb (more)	**mas**	conjunction (but)
mí	pronoun object of a preposition	**mi**	possessive pronoun
sí	reflexive pronoun or affirmative (yes)	**si**	conjunction (if)
sé	present indicative, **saber** or imperative of **ser**	**se**	reflexive pronoun
sólo	adverb (only)	**solo**	adjective (only, sole)
té	(tea)	**te**	personal pronoun
tú	subject pronoun (you)	**tu**	possessive adjective

PITFALL

A number of Spanish words may have two forms of accentuation. Some of the more common examples are:

celtíbero	**celtibero**
cónclave	**conclave**
dominó	**domino**
elíxir	**elixir**
médula	**medula**
orgía	**orgia**
présago	**presago**
utopía	**utopia**
várice	**varice**
vídeo (Spain)	**video (Latin America)**

DIALECTS AND VARIATIONS OF SPANISH AND OTHER IBERIAN LANGUAGES

In the early stages of language learning, dialectical and regional peculiarities are not a principal concern, and problems of this sort are usually explained in footnotes when they occur in textbooks. However, an awareness of the types of language differences that exist in peninsular Spain as well as the regional variations that occur in the

Spanish-speaking nations of the Western Hemisphere can aid in a more sensitive approach to writing and speaking Spanish even at the elementary level.

THE LANGUAGES OF SPAIN

Castilian

The speech of the educated residents of Madrid, Spain's capital city, has generally been considered a model of correct usage in peninsular Spanish (frequently called *castellano* rather than *español,* since it had its beginnings in the north central part of Spain known as Castilla.) Although Castilian is the official language of all Spain, many thousands of Spanish citizens do not speak it as a first language, and a few do not speak it at all.

Catalán, Gallego, and Basque have acquired new cultural importance as well as legal recognition in contemporary Spain, and television channels exist for programming in these regional languages.

Catalán

In Barcelona and the province of Catalonia, Catalán is spoken along with Spanish; business is conducted in the local language, and it is heard everywhere in conversation and in songs. Further evidence of the presence of a distinctive Catalán culture can be found in bookstores where original works in Catalán and American or European novels and plays translated into that language are sold. It should be remembered that Catalán is *not* a dialect of Spanish but another related Romance language like French, Portuguese, and Italian. A speaker of Spanish cannot automatically understand the language of Catalonia any more than a speaker of Italian can understand Portuguese. A brief comparison of a few lines in Catalán with the Spanish translation will illustrate some of the differences between the two languages.

Catalán:

> *Fa uns quants anys, pocs, Raimon irrompé dins la vida catalana com una veu jove, forta i sorprenentment autèntica. L'adhesió del públic fou immediate i entusiasta.*

Spanish:

> *Hare unos años, pocos, Raimon irrumpió en la vida catalana como una voz joven, fuerte y sorprendentemente auténtica. La adhesión del público fue inmediata y entusiástica.*

Valencian

In the province of Valencia there are many speakers of Valencian (el valencià), which is similar to Catalán (but a separate tongue in the opinion of the Valencians themselves). Although Valencian cannot claim the cultural importance of Catalán, it is, nevertheless, the regional dialect of a large and influential Spanish province, and examples of the language can be found in novels, short stories, and essays dealing with the life and customs of the area.

> —*¡Lladre! ¡Més que lladre!*—rugían mirando al tío *Sento*.
> (—¡Ladrón! ¡Más que ladrón!—)
> —*¡No vullc, no vullc!*—gritaba con angustia la
> (—¡No quiero, no quiero!—)
> muchacha—*¡Fuixca!*
>   (¡Huya!)

(Lines from "*La cencerrada*" by Vicente Blasco Ibáñez)

Galician

In northwestern Spain the regional language is Galician (or *gallego*), which shows a kinship with Portuguese. Non-Galician writers have on occasion cultivated the language because of its supposed superiority to Castilian for lyric poetry. The most notable example of literature written in Galician in modern times is the work of the poetess Rosalía de Castro (1837–1885) who wrote in both her regional language and in Spanish.

Galician: ***Ben sei que non hay nada***
novo en baixo d'o ceo,
qu'antes outros pensaron
as cousas qu'hora eu penso.
(Lines from "Vaguedas," in "Follas novas" by
Rosalía de Castro)

Spanish: **Bien sé que no hay nada**
nuevo bajo el cielo,
que antes otros pensaron
las cosas que ahora yo pienso.

Basque

The most unusual language of the Iberian peninsula is Basque (called
vascuence or *éuscaro* by the Spanish). Unlike Spanish and the other
southern European languages, Basque has no relationship to Latin
except in certain words borrowed from Spanish. It is notoriously difficult to learn, and the natives of the Basque territories in northern
Spain have long been known for their reluctance to be completely
assimilated into the national culture. Yet some of Spain's greatest
writers (Miguel de Unamuno, Pío Baroja) who were masters of
Castilian, were of Basque origin.

Caló

Caló is the language of Spain's Gypsy minority and is related to
Sanskrit. Although its grammatical structure is borrowed from
Spanish, its vocabulary is distinctive with a mixture of "gitano puro"
and words of Latin origin. Many Caló words can be found in Spanish
slang or argot, especially in southern Spain and in such professions as
bullfighting and flamenco dancing. Numerous Caló sayings or
"refranes" have been collected.

Caló: **Gres sos tué romandiñelas, diquela sosque**
querelas.
Spanish: **Antes que te cases, mira lo que haces.**

English:	Before you marry, look at what you're doing. (Look before you leap.)
Caló:	**Coín baribú sorna flimé trequejena.**
Spanish:	**Quien mucho duerme, poco aprende.**
English:	The one who sleeps a lot learns little.

DIALECTS OF SPANISH

As is the case with the English spoken in the United States, there are regional peculiarities of Spanish that immediately mark the place of origin of the speaker. Dialectical distinctions for the Spanish spoken in León, Aragón, Murcia, Andalucía, the Canary Islands, and other areas have been documented. Andalusian Spanish is perhaps the most colorful. Just as the southern American accent is frequently mimicked in motion pictures and on television and radio for humorous effect, the special accent of southern Spain is at times a source of humor in Spanish dramatic writings.

THE SPANISH OF THE NEW WORLD

Although Castilian is understood by all educated people in the Spanish-speaking nations of the New World, striking regional differences in vocabulary, accent, and usage can be noted. In some areas, essentially "pure" Spanish is flavored by many words drawn from the languages spoken by the Indian peoples whose civilizations developed before the arrival of the *conquistadores*. Some of these Indian words have become a part of international Spanish, and from Spanish have passed into English and other languages.

For example: *maíz*—corn, *tomate*—tomato, *huracán*—hurricane, *canoa*—canoe)

In the Caribbean island countries, including Puerto Rico, and in the countries of Central America, Spanish shows racial and cultural influences that are as important as those that can be distinguished in the larger nations. Probably the most striking structural differences are evident in the Spanish of the Río de la Plata region, which includes both Argentina and Uruguay. A distinctive form of the second person pronoun is used in place of *tú* (you—familiar). This form (*vos*) should not be confused with the plural *vosotros*, which is generally replaced by *ustedes* in the Spanish of the New World. The usual second person singular verb endings show a special modification in the present indicative and present subjunctive tenses. (Other tenses are not affected.)

Present Indicatives—ar, er, and ir verbs

vos cantás = **tú cantas**
vos vendés = **tú vendes**
vos escribís = **tú escribes**
and
vos sos = **tú eres**

Present Subjunctive

vos cantés = **tú cantes**
vos vendás = **tú vendas**
vos escribás = **tú escribas**

PITFALL

Radical or stem-changing verbs do not show the normal second person change, since the stress is on the ending as with the second person plural forms.

vos volvés = **tú vuelves** (Pres. Ind.)
vos volvás = **tú vuelvas** (Pres. Subj.)

PITFALL

The affirmative command forms for *vos* are the same as those for *vosotros* with the final *d* dropped and an accent added to the final syllable.

| *cantá* | rather than | **cantad** |
| *volvé* | rather than | **volved** |

PITFALL

The negative commands are the same as the present subjunctive forms for *vos*, or the normal *tú* form may be used.

| **no cantés** | or | **no cantes** |
| **no volvás** | or | **no vuelvas** |

THE SPANISH OF THE PHILIPPINES

The Philippine Islands were for a long period a colony of Spain, and the ruling class spoke Spanish. Philippine Spanish has a strong Mexican influence because the first expeditions to the islands departed from Mexico. In spite of a strong effect on the local speech, Spanish never supplanted the native Tagala (or Tagalog). After the war with the United States in 1898, when Spain lost control of the islands, the Spanish influence waned.

JUDEO-ESPAÑOL

In many parts of the world, especially the southern Mediterranean area, the descendants of the Sephardic Jews who were expelled from Spain by Ferdinand and Isabella in 1492, speak a Spanish that has retained the flavor of the language of the fifteenth century—even though these Jewish groups are far removed in time and space from the adopted homeland of their ancestors.

13 Special Aids

TIPS ON EVERYDAY USAGE
SPANISH ABBREVIATIONS
(ABREVIATURAS ESPAÑOLAS)

Abbreviations are essentially a carryover from the days when everything had to be written in longhand. With the advent of the typewriter—and now especially with copying devices such as photostats, photocopiers, and computer printers—the need for abbreviations is fast dying out. And there is no point in including in a modern listing such abbreviations as Q.B.S.P. (*que besa sus pies*—who kisses your feet) or V.A. (*Vuestra Alteza*—Your Highness). Any standard dictionary has such listings of obsolete expressions; and business abbreviations—those still in use—can be found in any manual of commercial correspondence. They would serve no useful purpose in a text such as this.

A
A.C., A. de C, Año de Cristo   A.D.
a/c, al cuidado   c/o (care of)
adj., adjunto   enclosure, enclosed
afmo., afectísimo suyo   yours very sincerely
a. de J.C., antes de Jesucristo   B.C.
apdo., apartado (de correos)   Post Office Box
Av., Av^da^, avenida   avenue

B
B., Beato   Blessed
B.A., Buenos Aires   (capital of Argentina)

C

c., capítulo   chapter
C., compañía   company
cap., capítulo   chapter
C. de J., Compañía de Jesús   S.J. (Society of Jesus)
c.f., caballo de fuerza   horsepower
cg., centigramo   centigram
Cía, compañía   company
cm., centímetro   centimeter
cm^2, centímetro cuadrado   square centimeter
cm^3, centímetro cúbico   cubic centimeter

D

D., Don   title of courtesy for men (*Sr.D.* when used before first name in an address)
D^a., Doña   title of courtesy for women (used only with first names)
d. de J.C., después de Jesucristo   A.D.
D.F. Distrito Federal (México)   Federal District
D.m., Dios mediante   God willing
doc., docena   dozen
Dr., Doctor   doctor

E

E., este   East(ern)
EE.UU., E.U.A., Estados Unidos   U.S., United States
esq. esquina   corner
etc., etcétera   etc.

F

f., femenino   feminine
f.c., ferrocarril   railroad
Fr., Fray   Friar, Brother

G

g/, giro   draft, money order
gr., grs., gramo(s)   gram(s)
Gral., general   General

H

hect., hectárea   hectare
Hno(s)., Hermano(s)   Brother(s)

I
igl.ª, iglesia   church
Ing., ingeniero   (title given to) engineer
IVA, impues to sobre el valor añadido   VAT (value-added tax)
izq.ª, izq.º, izq.ᵈᵃ, izq.ᵈᵒ, izquierda, izquierdo   left

J
J.C., Jesucristo   Jesus Christ

K
k/c., kilociclos   kilocycles
kg., kilogramo   kilogram
km./h., kilómetros por hora   kilometers per hour

L
l., litro   liter
Lic., licenciado   (title given to) lawyer
Lic. en Fil. y Let., Licenciado en Filosofía y Letras   Master of Arts

M
m., masculino   masculine
m., metro   meter
m., minuto   minute
m., murió   died
m², metro cuadrado   square meter
m³, metro cúbico   cubic meter
M.ª, María   (baptismal name) Mary
mg., miligramo   milligram
mm., milímetro   millimeter

N
n., nacido   born
N., norte   North(ern)
N.ª S.ª, Nuestra Señora   Our Lady (The Virgin Mary)
N.B., nótese bien   N.B. (nota bene)
N.S., Nuestro Señor   Our Lord
núm., número   number

O

O., oeste   West(ern)
ob., obpo., obispo   bishop
O.E.A., Organización de los Estados Americanos   O.A.S.
  (Organization of American States)
ONU, Organización de las Naciones Unidas   UN (United Nations)
OTAN, Organización del Tratado del Atlántico del Norte   NATO
  (North Atlantic Treaty Organization)

P

P., Padre   Father
pág., págs., página(s)   page(s)
P.D., posdata   P.S. (at end of letter)
p. ej., por ejemplo   e.g., for example
Prof., profesor   professor
ptas., pesetas   pesetas

Q

q.e.g.e., que en gloria esté   R.I.P. (used in obituaries)
q.e.p.d., que en paz descanse   R.I.P. (used in obituaries)
q.e.s.m., que estrecha su mano   Yours very truly

R

R., Reverendo   Reverend
RENFE, Red Nacional de Ferrocarriles Españoles
  (Spanish National Railways)
R.M.. Reverenda Madre   Reverend Mother
R.P., Reverendo Padre   Reverend Father

S

S., San(to), Santa   Saint
S., sur   South(ern)
S.A., Sociedad Anónima   Inc. (Incorporated)
s.f., sin fecha   no date
SIDA síndrome de inmunodeficiencia adquirida AIDS
Sr., Señor   Mr.
Sra., Señora   Mrs.
S.R.C., se ruega contestación   R.S.V.P.
Sres., Señores   Messrs.
Srta., Señorita   Miss

S.S., Su Santidad   His Holiness
s.s.s., su seguro servidor   Yours truly

T
t., tomo(s)   volume(s)
Tel., teléfono   telephone
T.L.C., Tratado de Libre Comercio   North American Free Trade Agreement (NAFTA)
T.V.E., Televisión Española   Spanish National Television

U
Ud., usted   you (singular)
Uds., ustedes   you (plural)

V
v., voltio   volt
v., véase   see
Vd., usted   you (singular)
Vda. de, viuda de   widow of
Vds., ustedes   you (plural)
vid., vide   see

LETTER WRITING

There are many ways in which a letter may be written in Spanish. In business letters, the Spanish are much more formal than Americans.

Openings and Closings

	Business Letters
Sample salutations:	**Muy distinguida señorita** **Muy señor mío** **Estimado profesor**
Complimentary closes:	**Quedo su atento y seguro servidor** (I remain yours truly) **Le saluda atentamente,** (signature) **Queda a su disposición,** (signature)

Letters to Friends and Relatives

Salutations:	**Querida Juana** **Querido amigo mío** **Queridísima mamá**
Complimentary Closes:	**Un abrazo de tu hijo (amigo, amiga)** **Con todo el cariño de** **Con cariño, tu amiga** **Afectuosamente** **Abrazos** (among friends)

Addressing a Letter

In Spanish the number of the house follows the street name. In Spain the postal code precedes the name of the city (28004 Madrid).

> Sr. Vicente Tovar
> Calle Obregón, 64
> Apto. C
> Guadalajara, Jalisco
> México

Useful Phrases for Letter Writing

Apartado postal (Apdo.)	Post Office Box
Certificada	Registered letter
Cía (Compañía)	Company
Correo aéreo	Air Mail
Lista de correos	General Delivery
Por avión	Air Mail
S.A. (Sociedad Anónima)	Comparable to English *Inc.* (Incorporated)
Urgente	Special Delivery

TELEPHONE CONVERSATIONS

When answering the telephone, the Spanish speaker may say *Diga*, *Dígame*, *Oigame*, *Bueno* or even *Aló* instead of "Hello." To ask for someone on the telephone, it is common to say "*¿Está el Sr.*

Martínez?" If the person being called has answered the phone, he would say "*Al habla*" or "*Soy yo*" to mean "speaking." In order to identify himself, the caller would say "*Habla el Sr. Ortega*" or "*Soy el Sr. Ortega.*" If the person answering the phone wants to know who is calling, he normally says "*¿De parte de quién?*"

Words for Telephone Use

colgar	to hang up
descolgar	to pick up the receiver
disco	dial
llamar	to call
marcar	to dial a phone number
número equivocado	wrong number
señal, tono	dial tone
sonar	to ring
poner (or **hacer**) **una teleconferencia**	to set up a teleconference

TIPS ON VOCABULARY BUILDING

COGNATE WORDS *(PALABRAS COGNADAS)*

The single most useful aid in vocabulary building is learning to recognize **cognates**—words in one language that have an identical or similar counterpart in the second language. Spanish and English have a great number of similar words, and although some of these may be deceptive and have a different meaning in one language or the other, most cognates are close in meaning in both languages.

Some of these pairs of words represent direct borrowings (and not all the English words currently in use in Spanish are necessarily sanctioned by the *Real Academia Española*).

Borrowings

English borrowing	Spanish borrowing
patio	**el bar**
vista	**el biftec**

| rodeo | **el suspense** (or **suspenso**) |
| tortilla | **el estrés** (from *stress*) |

A great many cognates or near cognates in Spanish and English are the result of a common kinship with Latin. In other cases they represent common borrowings from other languages.

Cognates

English	Spanish
attractive	**atractivo**
confusion	**confusión**
conversation	**conversación**
escape	**escape**
invisible	**invisible**
possible	**posible**
radical	**radical**
reality	**realidad**
Soviet	**soviet**
terrible	**terrible**
universal	**universal**
urgency	**urgencia**
and many others	

FALSE COGNATES OR "FALSE FRIENDS" (*FALSOS AMIGOS*)

False cognates are words in one language that are identical or very similar to words in a second language, but whose meanings are different. These are sometimes called "false friends" because they are recognizable in form but undependable in meaning.

False Friends

Spanish—English	English—Spanish
actual, present-day	actual, **real, efectivo**
agonía, death struggle	agony, **angustia**

Spanish—English

apología, eulogy, defense
arena, sand
asistir, to attend (e.g., school)
atender, to take care of or attend to
bizarro, gallant, brave,
generous, liberal
campo, country
carta, letter
cimiento, foundation, root origin
complexión, constitution,
temperament
confección, handiwork,
fancy work
conferencia, lecture
decepción, disappointment
delito, crime
desgracia, misfortune
desmayo, faint
editor, publisher
embarazada, pregnant
emocionante, thrilling
éxito, success
fábrica, factory
faltar, to be lacking
gracioso, funny
ignorar, to not know something
injuria, injustice, damage, harm
jubilación, retirement, pension
largo, long
marca, brand (of a product)
marco, picture frame
once, eleven
ordinario, common, vulgar
pan, bread
pariente, relative
quitar, to take away, remove
realizar, to achieve a goal

English—Spanish

apology, **excusa**
arena, **estadio, coliseo**
assist, **ayudar**
attend, **asistir**
bizarre, **raro, original**

camp, **campamento**
card, **tarjeta**
cement, **cemento**
complexion, **tez**

confection, **pastel**

conference, **consulta**
deception, **engaño**
delight, **deleite**
disgrace, **vergüenza**
dismay, **consternación**
editor, **redactor**
embarrassing, **embarazoso**
emotional, **emocional**
exit, **salida**
fabric, **tejido**
fault, **culpa**
gracious, **cortés**
ignore, **no hacer caso de**
injury, **daño, herida**
jubilation, **júbilo**
large, **grande**
mark, **señal**

once, **una vez**
ordinary, **común, corriente**
pan, **sartén**
parent, **padre o madre**
quit, **dejar**
realize, **darse cuenta de**

Spanish—English	English—Spanish
recolección, compilation, summary	recollection, **recuerdo, memoria**
red, net	red, **rojo**
restar, deduct	rest, **descansar**
sano, healthy	sane, **cuerdo**
sentencia, verdict, judgment	sentence, **frase**
simpático, appealing, pleasant	sympathetic, **compasivo**
suceso, event, happening	success, **éxito**
trampa, cheat	tramp, **vagabundo**

PREFIXES

A familiarity with the meaning of Spanish prefixes can be a valuable aid to building a larger vocabulary. Attention should be given to the change in meaning that a root word acquires when different prefixes are used.

poner,	to put, place
deponer	depose
disponer	dispose
entreponer	interpose
exponer	expose, show
imponer	impose
interponer	interpose
posponer	postpone
proponer	propose
reponer	replace
sobreponer	superimpose
superponer	superimpose

Common Prefixes

ab-, abs-	privation or separation
abstener	to abstain
abdicar	to abdicate

ad-, a-	in the direction of, toward
adyacente, adjacent	
acercar, to bring near, to approach	

an-, a-	privation or negation **anormal,** abnormal **analfabeto,** illiterate
ante-	before **anteayer,** the day before yesterday **antemano,** beforehand, in advance **antebrazo,** forearm **anteanoche,** the night before last **antecesor,** ancestor
anti-	opposition to **anticonstitucional,** unconstitutional **anticongelante,** antifreeze
bis-, biz-, bi-	twice or double **bisabuelo,** great-grandfather
circun-	around **circunlocución,** talking around the subject **circunscribir,** to circumscribe
con-, co-	with, together, jointly **confraternidad,** confraternity, brotherhood **condominio,** joint ownership **colaborar,** to work together with someone else **condiscípulo,** fellow student
contra-	opposition to **contradecir,** contradict **contracorriente,** cross current
des-, de-	privation, negation or separation **deshacer,** to undo; to take apart, to wear away **degenerar,** to degenerate **demérito,** demerit **desesperar,** to lose hope **desaparecer,** to disappear
dis-, di	take apart or separate; deprive of, exclude or expel from **disculpar,** to excuse, to pardon **disgregar,** to break up, to disintegrate

disidir, to dissent

en-   interior, place in which, acquisition of a quality
enjaular, to cage up
enflaquecer, to get thin
engordar, to fatten, to get fat

entre-   between
entreacto, intermission
entremezclar, to intermingle
entremeter, to insert, to intrude

ex-, es-, e-   direction toward, outside, privation, end of duty
or responsibility
exportar, to export
ex-presidente, ex-president
exponer, to expose

extra-   outside of
extraordinario, extraordinary
extracurricular, extracurricular

hiper-   superiority or excess
hipercrítico, hypercritical
hipertensión, hypertension
hipersensible, hypersensitive

in-, i-   negation, or place in which
ilógico, illogical
ilegal, illegal
imponer, impose

inter-   between, among, in the midst of
interceder, to intercede
interacción, interaction
intercambiar, to interchange

pos-, post-   afterwards
posponer, to postpone
posguerra, postwar
posdata, postscript
póstumo, posthumous

pre-	prior to, preparatory or prerequisite to **presuponer,** to presuppose **predilección,** predilection
pro-	before or instead of **pronombre,** pronoun **prólogo,** prologue **prominente,** prominent
re-	repetition, intensity, or step backwards **rehacer,** to do over, to mend **reponer,** to replace, to restore **reconocer,** to recognize, to admit **reaccionar,** to react
sobre-	superiority or excess **sobrehombre,** superman **sobresalir,** to stand out, to project **sobrepasar,** to surpass
sub-, so-	underneath **subterráneo,** underground **submarino,** submarine **socavar,** to dig under, to undermine
super-	superiority or excess **superponer,** to superimpose **superabundancia,** superabundance

SUFFIXES

The number of suffixes that Spanish and English have in common is very great, but the student should not be lulled into a false sense of security. Since the patterns cited to not apply to every word, these suffixes are included for recognition purposes while reading literature in Spanish and *not* necessarily for word formation when writing in the language.

It is noteworthy how many different words can be formed from one word, the root word. Following are two examples.

The Addition of Suffixes

joya	jewel
joyero	jeweler
joyería	jewelry shop
joyera	jewelry box

pelo	hair
pelirrojo	red-haired
pelón	bald
peloso	hairy
peluca	wig
peludo	hairy
peluquería	barber shop or beauty shop
peluquero	barber or hairdresser

Common Suffixes

SPANISH NOUN SUFFIXES AND ENGLISH EQUIVALENTS

-acio	(ace)	**prefacio,** preface
-ador	(ator)	**senador,** senator
-aje	(age)	**follaje,** foliage
-al	(al)	**canal,** canal
-ante	(ant)	**coagulante,** coagulant
-ente	(ent)	**continente,** continent
-gio	(ge)	**prestigio,** prestige
-ía	(y)	**biología,** biology
-icio	(ice)	**precipicio,** precipice
-ista	(ist)	**artista,** artist
-mento	(ment)	**monumento,** monument
-or	(or)	**actor,** actor
-tro	(ter)	**teatro,** theater
-ura	(ure)	**conjetura,** conjecture

ABSTRACT NOUN SUFFIXES

-ancia	(ance)	**fragancia,** fragrance
-cia	(cy)	**necromancia,** necromancy

-ción	(tion)	**educación,** education
-cto	(ct)	**acto,** act
-dad	(ty)	**ciudad,** city
-encia	(ence or ency)	**contingencia,** contingency
-ica	(ic)	**música,** music
-ina	(ine)	**medicina,** medicine
-ión	(ion)	**religión,** religion
-ismo	(ism)	**comunismo,** Communism
-tud	(tude)	**actitud,** attitude

ADJECTIVE SUFFIXES

-az	(acious)	**vivaz,** vivacious
-al	(al)	**nacional,** national
-ano	(an)	**americano,** American
-ante	(ant)	**predominante,** predominant
-ar	(ar)	**lunar,** lunar
-ario	(ary)	**contrario,** contrary
-ble	(ble)	**formidable,** formidable
-cial	(tial)	**esencial,** essential
-ente	(ent)	**permanente,** permanent
-ito	(ite)	**infinito,** infinite
-ivo	(ive)	**pasivo,** passive
-no	(nal)	**materno,** maternal
-oso	(ous)	**famoso,** famous
-uro	(ure)	**futuro,** future

SUFFIXES OF NATIONALITY

Six different suffixes indicate nationality or geographical origin. There are no set rules for which suffix to use for any given country or region. The dictionary should be consulted.

-ano	**sevillano, asturiano**
-ense	**costarricense, estadounidense**
-eño	**madrileño, extremeño**
-és	**francés, inglés, portugués**
-í	**marroquí**
-ino	**salmantino**

SUFFIXES WITH SPECIAL MEANINGS

-ada This suffix can sometimes be equivalent to the English -ful or can denote a capacity of something.
una cucharada   a teaspoonful

The suffix can also refer to some kind of blow or a crowd of people.
una puñada   a punch
una cuchillada   a slash with a knife

-ada, -ida Occasionally the feminine singular form of the past participle is used to form a noun from a verb.
salir   **salida,** exit
ir   **ida,** departure
llegar   **llegada,** arrival

-ado, -ato This suffix is derived from nouns of title or address and denotes jurisdiction.
califa   **califato,** caliphate
papa   **papado,** papacy

-aje A word ending in -*aje* may sometimes refer to a fee exacted, or a group of persons.
puente   **pontaje,** bridge toll
gaucho   **gauchaje,** group of gauchos

-al or **-ar** denotes a grove, field or plantation.
naranjal   orange grove
cafetal   coffee plantation
pinar   pine grove
olivar   olive grove

-ante often a suffix of profession or job.
comerciante   businessman
estudiante   student

-azo indicates a blow with an object. The object is found in the root word.

bala	**balazo,** a bullet wound
codo	**codazo,** a jab with the elbow
látigo	**latigazo,** whiplash

-dizo added to some adjectives to form a word that describes what someone or something is like.

enojadizo	irritable, easily annoyed
bebedizo	drinkable

-eda, -edo denotes the place where a thing grows.

árbol	**arboleda,** grove
álamo	**alameda,** grove of poplars

-eño adjectives formed from a noun, denoting likeness.

águila	**aguileño,** aquiline
risa	**risueño,** smiling

-era sometimes added to a noun to denote that which it contains.

leche	**lechera,** milk pitcher
café	**cafetera,** coffee pot

-ería can indicate a place where something is made or sold.

libro	**librería,** bookstore
hierro	**ferretería,** hardware store
zapato	**zapatería,** shoe store

can also refer to a profession or occupation.
ingeniería, engineering

-ero This suffix can have many meanings. It may be used to form the word for a container or can refer to the operator of a store.

grano	**granero,** granary
pelo	**peluquero,** barber
zapato	**zapatero,** shoemaker

-ero can also be used to form adjectives which give a characteristic, e.g. *guerrero*, warlike and *parlero*, talkative.

-ez, -eza	These suffixes form abstract nouns.

viejo	**vejez,** old age
niño	**niñez,** childhood
bajo	**bajeza,** lowliness
triste	**tristeza,** sadness

-ía, ia	a suffix that commonly refers to one of the humanities or sciences.

geografía	geography
biología	biology
historia	history

From names of sciences and the humanities that end in *ía*, the professional man's title may be obtained by changing the *ía* to *o*.

biología	**biólogo,** biologist
fotografía	**fotógrafo,** photographer
filosofía	**filósofo,** philosopher

-iento	tells of a characteristic or something or to be like the root word.

ceniza, ash	**ceniciento,** ashen
hambre, hunger	**hambriento,** starving

-ísimo	ending of the absolute superlative.

mucho	**muchísimo,** very much
hermoso	**hermosísimo,** exceedingly beautiful

-izo	means *somewhat like* the root word.

rojo	**rojizo,** reddish
enfermo	**enfermizo,** sickly

| **-mente** | the adverbial ending attached to the feminine singular adjective. |
| | **cuidadosa**   **cuidadosomente,** carefully |

-mento,	used to form abstract nouns from verbs.
-miento	**conocer** **conocimiento,** knowledge
	sentir **sentimiento,** feeling

-udo	can form adjectives that express a quality of the root word (noun) from which they are formed.
	barba **barbudo,** heavy-bearded
	hueso **huesudo,** big-boned

-ura	forms abstract nouns from adjectives.
	blanco **blancura,** whiteness
	alto **altura,** height
	bravo **bravura,** braveness

PITFALL

Note that names of fruit trees ending in -o can be changed to mean the names of the fruits substituting an -a for the -o.

manzano, apple tree	**manzana,** apple
naranjo, orange tree	**naranja,** orange
cerezo, cherry tree	**cereza**, cherry

AUGMENTATIVES AND DIMINUTIVES

An **augmentative** is a suffix that indicates large size and sometimes awkwardness or unattractiveness. A **diminutive** indicates small size and sometimes the quality of being lovable, or subject to scorn.

PITFALL

Words with diminutive and augmentative endings frequently do not have a single, special meaning. Many times a speaker will use an augmentative or diminutive word with ironic intent. In English a mother will say to her little boy after he has done something well: That's a big boy!" The Spanish sometimes speak this way also. An examination of the context in which the word occurs or the intonation that the speaker uses will help determine if there is an ironic meaning.

PITFALL

Some words with an apparent diminutive or augmentative ending now have a single basic dictionary meaning.

hermanastro (a)	stepbrother (stepsister)
sillón	armchair
panecillo	roll
señorita	Miss
and others	

PITFALL

The augmentative and diminutive suffixes can be used with nouns as well as adjectives, adverbs, present participles (*gerundio*) and past participles.

calladito	very quietly
cerquita	very close
ahorita mismo	right this very minute
or	
ahora mismito	
sentadito	sitting prim and proper

Augmentative Suffixes

───────────── RULE ─────────────

The most common augmentative endings are: *acho*, *azo*, *ón*, and *ote* with their various corresponding feminine and plural forms.
The ending -*ón* is the most common and usually indicates large size.

Quiero un cucharón para batir los ingredients.
I want a big spoon to beat the ingredients.

PITFALL

The endings *acho*, *azo*, and *ote,* besides indicating large size, sometimes convey the idea of ridiculousness, monstrosity or disproportion. Some words of this type are insulting or offensive.

Juan es un grandote.
John is a big guy.

Esa señora es una madraza.
That lady is an overly indulgent mother.

No se permiten palabrotas aquí.
Obscenities are not permitted here.

Diminutive Suffixes

── RULE ──

The most common diminutive endings are: *-ico*, *-illo*, *-ito*, and *-uelo*. Other less common diminutive suffixes are: *-ín*, *-ino*, *-iño*, *ete*, *-ajo*, *-ejo*, and *-ijo*.

Juanito recibió un perrito para su cumpleaños.
Johnny received a puppy for his birthday.

—Paco, ven acá.   —Momentico mamá.
"Paco, come here."   "Just a minute, Mother."

Aquí se venden bocadillos.
Sandwiches (little mouthfuls) are sold here.

Ellos prefieren pescar en el arroyuelo.
They prefer fishing in the little stream.

Pejorative Suffixes

Words with the following suffixes usually have a derogatory meaning.

-acho, populacho	mob, rabble
-aco, libraco	trashy book
-ajo, comistrajo	hodgepodge, mess
-astro, poetastro	inferior poet
-ejo, librejo	worthless book
-oste, armatoste	fat, clumsy fellow
-ote, monigote	grotesque figure
-ucho, avechucho	ugly bird, ragamuffin
-uco, mujeruca	slovenly woman
-uzo, gentuza	rabble, mob

PITFALL

All diminutives and augmentatives should be used with great care; you may easily insult someone by choosing the wrong suffix.

WORDS FREQUENTLY CONFUSED

While one English word can have many meanings, Spanish may use several different words. A dictionary listing of *fair* gives a good idea of how many Spanish words may translate as *fair* in English. Notice that each Spanish word has a special restricted meaning.

fair adj. 1. (handsome; comely) hermoso; bello 2. (blond) rubio 3. (light-skinned) blanco; de tez blanca 4. (unblemished) intachable; limpio 5. (just; honest) justo; recto 6. (valid) legal; válido 7. (clear; sunny) claro; despejado 8. (good; of good size or quality) buen; bueno 9. (average) regular; pasable.

Again	**otra vez:** again (repetition).
	Dígalo *otra vez.*
	Say it again.

de nuevo: over again (from the beginning).
Trata de hacerlo *de nuevo.*
Try to do it again.

volver a + infinitive: to do something again.
Volvió a **decir lo mismo.**
He said the same thing again.

Appear

aparecer: to appear (in the physical sense).
De repente, José *apareció* **a la puerta.**
Suddenly, José appeared at the door.

parecer: to seem, to appear (in the figurative sense).
Ella *parecía* **divertirse.**
She seemed to enjoy herself.

Ask

preguntar: to ask a question.
Él me *preguntó* **dónde estaba el centro.**
He asked me where downtown was.

pedir: to request; to ask for something.
Ellos *pidieron* **unas Cocas al camarero.**
They asked the waiter for some Cokes.

Become

hacerse: to become (physical change); to become (enter a profession)
Carlos *se hizo* **médico.** Carlos became a doctor.

ponerse: to become (condition or state).
Yo *me puse* **pálida al oír las noticias.**
I became pale when I heard the news.

llegar a ser: to become (achieve after effort).
Llegará a ser **gran arquitecto.**
He will become a great architect.

Can

poder: to be physically able to; may (referring to permission).
Puede **levantar pesas de 200 libras.**
He can lift 200-pound weights.

saber: to know how to.
Ella *sabe* **tocar bien la guitarra.**
She can play the guitar well.

Character **personaje:** character (in a book or play).
Augusto Pérez es el *personaje* **más importante de la novela** *Niebla.*
Augusto Pérez is the most important character of the novel *Niebla*.

carácter: character (personal traits or attributes).
Tiene un *carácter* **muy bueno.**
He has a very good character

Commercial **anuncio:** advertisement, commercial (noun).
Los *anuncios* **de televisión insultan al público.**
Television commercials insult the public.

comercial: commercial (adj.); referring to commerce.
Es un asunto *comercial.*
It is a commercial affair.

Corner **rincón:** corner (indoors)
Ponga la lámpara en ese *rincón.*
Put the lamp in that corner.

esquina: corner (outdoors)
Ese guitarrista siempre toca en la *esquina* **de la Avenida Juárez.**
That guitarist always plays on the corner of Júarez Avenue.

Country **país:** country, nation.
México es un *país.*
Mexico is a country.

campo: country (opposite of city).
Prefiero vivir en el *campo* **que en la ciudad.**
I would rather live in the country than in the city.

patria: fatherland, native land.
La *patria* de José Martí es Cuba.
José Martí's native land is Cuba.

Go   **ir:**   to go.
Vamos al teatro esta noche.
We're going to the theater tonight.

irse: to go away.
¡Véte!
Scram!

salir: to go out, leave.
Salió hace cinco minutos.
He left five minutes ago.

bajar: to go down.
Bajó la escalera.
He went down the stairs.

subir: to go up
Subió la escalera.
He went up the stairs.

Grass   **hierba:**   grass, herb.

pasto: pasture.

césped: lawn, sod.

Hear   **oír:**   to hear (perceive sound).
Oigo un ruido.
I hear a noise.

escuchar: to listen to.
Me gusta *escuchar* esa música.
 I like to listen to that music

Know   **saber:**   to know (a fact); to know how to do something.
Yo *sé* ese poema de memoria.
I know that poem by heart.

Sabe divertirse.
He knows how to enjoy himself.

conocer: to know, be acquainted with (a person or a city).
Le *conozco.*
I know him.

El taxista *conoce* bien las calles de Guadalajara.
The taxi driver knows the streets of Guadalajara well.

Leave

salir: to leave, to go out
Ella *salió* del apartamento.
She left the apartment.

debar: to leave behind; to let, allow.
***Dejó* una propina para la camarera.**
He left a tip for the waitress.

Little

pequeño: little (size)
Prefiero un coche *pequeño.*
I prefer a small car.

poco: little (amount); similar to English prefix "un-".
Tiene *poca* inteligencia.
He has little intelligence.

Love, Like

querer: to love (a person)
Ella *quiere* a su esposo.
She loves her husband.

encantar: to love (a thing)
A ella le *encanta* la música de Granados.
She loves the music of Granados.

gustar: to like (person or thing)
A ella le *gusta* arroz con pollo.
She likes arroz con pollo.

¿Le *gusto* a ella?
Does she like me?

Make <u>hacer:</u> to make (something); *hacer* + infinitive: to make (someone) do something.
Ese señor *hace* huaraches.
That man makes sandals.

Nos *hizo* escribir una carta a mamá.
He made us write a letter to Mother.

<u>ganar:</u> to earn, make (money).
Gana **mucho más dinero que yo.**
He makes a lot more money than I do.

Miss <u>perder:</u> to miss (a train).
Perdí **el tren.**
I missed the train.

<u>echar de menos,</u> <u>extrañar:</u> to miss (a person or thing).
Te *echo de menos*.
I miss you. (Also: Te extraño.)

<u>faltar a:</u> to not be present for an occasion.
Faltó a **la fiesta.**
He missed the party.

Part <u>parte:</u> part (of the whole).
Ella quiere la tercera *parte* de la torta.
She wants a third of the cake.

<u>papel:</u> part, role.
Tiene el *papel* de Hamlet.
He has the part of Hamlet.

Party <u>fiesta:</u> party, celebration (social).
Voy a dar una *fiesta*.
I'm going to give a party.

<u>partido:</u> party (political organization).
Es un miembro del *partido* conservador.
He is a member of the Conservative Party.

Pay	**pagar:** to pay (money). *Paga* **tus deudas.** Pay your debts.
	prestar atención, hacer caso: to pay attention. **Estudiantes,** *presten atención,* **por favor.** Students, pay attention, please.
	Nunca *hace caso* **del programa.** He never pays attention to the program.
People	**gente:** people (in general).
	personas: persons (individuals).
	pueblo: the people (a race, nation).
Play	**jugar:** to play (a game, sport, cards). *Juega* **a las cartas cada sábado.** He plays cards every Saturday.
	tocar: to play (an instrument). *Toca* **el piano.** He plays the piano.
	hacer un papel: to play a role (part). *Hace el papel de Segismundo.* He plays the role of Segismundo.
Realize	**darse cuenta de:** to realize, to become aware of. **No** *me di cuenta de* **que tú estabas aquí.** I didn't realize that you were here.
	realizar: to achieve a goal. **Por fin José** *realizó* **su meta de hacerse abogado.** Finally José realized his goal of becoming a lawyer.
Return	**volver:** to come back. *Vuelve* **a casa a las 10 en punto.** Come back home at ten o'clock sharp.

devolver: to return (a thing).
Devuélvame **mi libro.**
Return my book.

Right **derecho:** right (law).
Ella tiene el *derecho* **de expresar su opinión.**
She has the right to express her opinion.

a la derecha: to the right, on the right (direction).
El museo está *a la derecha.*
The museum is to the right.

tener razón: to be right
Siempre dice que su amigo *tiene razón.*
He always says his friend is right.

Spend **gastar:** to spend (money).
Gastó **todo su dinero.**
He spent all his money.

pasar: to spend (time).
Pasé **dos horas en El Prado.**
I spent two hours in The Prado.

Surround **rodear:** to surround.
Estaba *rodeado* **de amigos.**
He was surrounded by friends.

cercar: to fence in; to surround.
Los prisioneros están *cercados* **en la estacada.**
The prisoners are surrounded in the stockade.

Take **llevar:** to take from one place to another, to take
a person.
Juan me *llevó* **a casa.**
Juan took me home.

tomar: to take, grasp; to eat or drink.
Quiero *tomar* **ese curso.**
I want to take that course.

sacar una foto: to take a picture.
Me gusta *sacar fotos*.
I like to take pictures.

dar un paseo: to take a walk.
Demos un paseo.
Let's take a walk.

There are many other verbs that translate "to take" in English. Check a dictionary for others.

The foregoing lists, while reasonably adequate for beginning and intermediate students, are by no means intended to be exhaustive. See the Bibliography for further treatment.

14 Specialized Vocabularies and Professional Terminology

The following vocabularies are provided to enable the inexperienced reader to quickly find useful and appropriate words for dealing with a number of professional, travel and emergency situations. However, they provide only an introduction to the terminology required for a professional level of fluency.

AIRLINES AND AIR TRAVEL

People

captain	**el capitán**
crewmember	**el tripulante**
passenger	**el pasajero, la pasajera**
pilot	**el piloto**
flight attendant,	**el ayudante de cabina,**
stewardess	**la azafata (*or* aeromoza)**

Actions

to fasten (seat belt)	**abrocharse (el cinturón)**
to land	**aterrizar**
to lift off	**despegar**
to make a stopover	**hacer escala**

Things

airline	**la línea aérea**
airplane	**el avión**
airport	**el aeropuerto**

altitude	**la altura**
claim check	**el comprobante**
emergency procedures	**los procedimientos de emergencia**
flight	**el vuelo**
jet engine	**el reactor, motor de reacción**
landing	**el aterrizaje**
liftoff	**el despegue**
meal	**la comida**
oxygen	**el oxígeno**
refreshment	**el refresco**
restrooms	**los servicios**
seat	**el asiento**
seat belt	**el cinturón**
speed	**la velocidad**
ticket	**el billete** (*or* **boleto**)

BANKING AND FINANCIAL TRANSACTIONS

People

banker	**el banquero**
cashier, teller	**el cajero, la cajera**
depositor	**el depositor, la depositora**
loan manager	**el (la) oficial de préstamos**
manager (of branch bank)	**el (la) gerente del sucursal**
public accountant (CPA)	**el contador público graduado**
programmer	**el programador**

Actions

to cash (a check)	**cobrar, hacer efectivo**
to deposit	**depositar**
to exchange (money)	**cambiar**
to sign, endorse	**firmar, endosar**

Things

ATM	**cajero automático**
bank	**el banco**
bankbook, passbook	**la libreta de depósito**
business (enterprise)	**la empresa (de negocios)**
check	**el cheque (certificado, de viajeros,** etc.**)**
coin	**la moneda**
compound interest	**interés compuesto**
computer	**la computadora (Latin America),**
	el ordenador (Spain)
credit card	**la tarjeta de crédito**
deposit	**el depósito**
foreign exchange	**las divisas**
income (salary)	**el ingreso, el sueldo**
interest	**el interés**
invoice	**la factura**
loan	**el préstamo**
mortgage	**la hipoteca**
photocopier	**la copiadora**
photocopy	**la fotocopia**
safe-deposit box	**la caja de seguridad**
savings	**los ahorros**
savings and loan	**caja de ahorros**
savings account	**la cuenta de ahorros**
securities	**los valores**
(stocks and bonds)	
tax	**el impuesto**
tax exemption	**la exención de impuestos**
typewriter	**la máquina de escribir**

COMPUTERS

People

programmer	**el programador (la programadora)**

Actions

to eject (a disk)	**expulsar (un disco)**
to install	**instalar**
to print	**imprimir**
to program	**programar**
to save (a file)	**guardar (un archivo)**

Things

computer	**la computadora, el ordenador**
data base	**la base de texto**
disk drive	**la disketera**
file, menu	**el archivo**
floppy disk	**el disco flexible**
hard disk	**el disco duro**
hardware	**el hardware**
keyboard	**el teclado**
laser printer	**la impresora láser**
memory	**la memoria**
modem	**el módem**
monitor	**el monitor**
mouse	**el ratón**
peripherals	**el equipo periférico**
portable computer	**la computadora portátil**
printer	**la impresora**
random access memory (RAM)	**la memoria RAM**
software	**el software**
spreadsheet	**la hoja de cálculo**
word processor	**el procesador de texto**

LAW AND LAW ENFORCEMENT

People

bank robber	**el atracador**
coroner	**el médico forense**
criminal	**el (la) criminal, el (la) reo**
defense attorney	**el defensor, la defensora**

district attorney, prosecutor	**el (la) fiscal**
drug addict	**el drogadicto, la drogadicta**
drug pusher	**el (la) traficante**
judge	**el (la) juez**
jury	**el jurado**
lawyer, attorney	**el (la) abogado**
policeman	**el policía**
police force	**la policía**
swindler	**el estafador, la estafadora**
terrorist	**el, la terrorista**
thief, robber	**el ladrón, la ladrona**

Actions

to arrest	**arrestar, detener**
to book	**fichar**
to fine	**multar, dar una multa**
to jail	**encarcelar**
to kidnap	**secuestrar, raptar**
to notarize	**legalizar, certificar**
to punish	**castigar**
to register (car, gun, etc.)	**matricular**
to report (a crime)	**denunciar, delatar**
to search	**registrar**
to sentence	**sentenciar**
to shoot	**disparar**
to testify	**atestiguar**

Things

courtroom	**la sala del tribunal**
crime	**el delito, el crimen**
injury, damage	**el agravio**
jail	**la cárcel, la prisión**
jail cell	**la celda**
law (profession)	**el derecho**

law (specific statute)	**la ley**
law office	**el bufete**
murder	**el homicidio**
penalty	**la pena**
police station	**la jefatura de policía**
rape	**la violación**
robbery	**el robo, el hurto**
traffic control	**el departamento de tránsito**
trial	**el juicio**
will	**el testamento**

MEDICINE AND HEALTH

People

dentist	**el (la) dentista**
doctor, physician	**el, la médico**
medical aide	**el, la ayudante**
medical technician	**el técnico, la técnica en medicina**
nurse	**la enfermera, el enfermero**
patient	**el, la paciente**
pharmacist	**el farmacéutico, la farmacéutica**
psychiatrist	**el (la) psiquiatra**
specialist	**el (la) especialista**
surgeon	**el (la) cirujano**

Actions

to bandage	**vendar**
to bleed	**sangrar**
to breathe	**respirar**
to choke	**atragantarse**
to cough	**toser**
to give a checkup	**hacer un examen**
to give a shot	**poner una inyección, inyectar**
to hurt	**doler (le) a uno**
to lose consciousness	**perder el conocimiento**
to suffer (from)	**padecer (de)**
to swell	**hinchar**

to take blood pressure	**tomar la presión**
to vaccinate	**vacunar**

Things

allergy	**la alergia**
antibiotic	**el antibiótico**
arthritis	**la artritis**
blood pressure	**la presión, la tensión**
break, fracture	**la fractura**
burn	**la quemadura**
cold	**el resfriado, el catarro**
cough	**la tos**
crutches	**las muletas**
doctor's office	**el consultorio, la clínica**
emergency room	**la sala de emergencia (urgencia)**
eyeglasses	**las gafas, los anteojos**
examination	**el examen físico**
fever	**la fiebre**
first aid	**los primeros auxilios**
form (medical)	**la planilla**
headache (migraine)	**la jaqueca**
hearing-aid	**el audífono**
heart attack	**el ataque cardíaco**
influenza	**la gripe**
injury	**la herida**
pacemaker	**el marcapasos**
pharmacy, drug store	**la farmacia**
pill, tablet	**la pastilla, el comprimido**
poisoning	**el envenenamiento**
prescription	**la receta**
stretcher	**la camilla**
waiting room	**la sala de espera**
X-Rays	**los rayos equis, la radiografía**

THEATER, TELEVISION, AND FILMS

People

actor	**el actor**
actress	**la actriz (las actrices)**
announcer	**el locutor, la locutora**
audience	**los espectadores, el público**
character (in a play, etc.)	**el personaje**
director (stage, film)	**el director**
dressing room	**el camarín**
manager (of theater company)	**el empresario**
playwright	**dramaturgo, dramaturga**
producer (TV)	**director de programación**
producer (stage)	**director de escena**
stagehand	**el tramoyista**
usher	**el acomodador**

Actions

to act	**actuar**
to applaud	**aplaudir**
to film	**filmar**
to open (play, film)	**estrenar**
to perform	**representar**
to play role (of)	**hacer el papel (de)**
to put on the air	**poner en antena**
to rehearse	**ensayar**
to televise	**televisar**

Things

box office	**la taquilla**
cast	**el elenco**
channel (TV)	**el canal**
close-up	**el gran primer plano**
commercial (TV)	**el anuncio comercial**

curtain	**el telón**
film	**la película, el filme**
microphone	**el micrófono**
newscast	**el noticiario, las noticias**
opening night	**el estreno**
opera house	**teatro de ópera**
orchestra seat	**la butaca**
performance	**la representación**
play	**la comedia, el drama**
role	**el papel**
screen	**la pantalla**
screenplay, teleplay	**el guión**
set (stage)	**el decorado**
stage	**el escenario**
teleplay	**la telecomedia**
television set	**el televisor**
theater (for plays)	**el teatro**
theater (for motion pictures)	**el cine**
theater ticket	**la entrada, el billete, el boleto**
video camera	**la videocámara**
videocassette	**el videocasete**
videotape	**la videocinta**
wings (of stage)	**los bastidores**

Bibliography

Casado, Manuel. *El castellano actual: usos y normas.* Cuarta edición revisada. Pamplona: Ediciones Universidad de Navarra, 1993.

Diez, Miguel, Francisco Morales, and Angel Sabin. *Las lenguas de España.* Madrid: Ministerio de Educación, Instituto Nacional de Ciencias de la Educación, 1980.

Dueber, Julianne. *Spanish Vocabulary.* New York: Barron's Educational Series, 1990.

Fontanella de Weinberg, María Beatriz. *El español de América.* Madrid: Editorial Mapfre, 1993.

García de Diego, Vicente. *Gramática histórica española.* Madrid: Editorial Gredos, 1961.

Langenscheidt's New College Spanish Dictionary. Berlin and Munich: Langenscheidt KG, 1995.

Lapesa, Rafael. *Historia de la lengua española.* Novena Edición. Madrid: Escelicer, S. A., 1980.

Larousse Spanish-English/English-Spanish Dictionary. Unabridged Edition. Paris: Larousse, 1993.

León, Víctor. *Diccionario de argot español.* Nueva edición ampliada. Madrid: Alianza Editorial, 1995.

Navarro Tomás, Tomás. *Manual de pronunciación española.* 19ª Edición. Madrid: Publicaciones de la Revista de Filología Española, 1977.

Politzer, Robert L. and Charles N. Staubach. *Teaching Spanish, A Linguistic Orientation.* Waltham, Massachusetts: Blaisdell Publishing Co., 1965.

Real Academia Española. *Diccionario de la lengua española.* 21ª Edición. Madrid: Espasa Calpe, 1992.

Seco, Manuel. *Gramática esencial del español*. Tercera edición. Madrid: Espasa Calpe, 1995.

Simon and Schuster's Diccionario internacional/International Dictionary. Edited by Tana de Gámez. New York: Simon and Schuster, 1973.

Spaulding, Robert K. *How Spanish Grew*. Berkeley: University of California Press, 1965.

Stockwell, Robert P., J. Donald Bowen and John W. Martin. *The Grammatical Structures of English and Spanish*. Chicago: University of Chicago Press, 1965.

Varela, Fernando and Hugo Kubarth. *Diccionario fraseológico del español moderno*. Madrid: Editorial Gredos, 1994.

Index

Notes

Notes

Notes

Notes

Notes

Notes

Notes

Notes

Notes

Notes